Advance Praise

"Engagingly, even delightfully written, *Giving with Confidence* deserves an immediate read by anyone interested in giving, givers, or improving our world. Part up-to-date behind-the-scenes guide, part how-to, this potent little book distills the wisdom of a life's work in philanthropy by one of our best thinkers and most devoted practitioners. Cole Wilbur unhesitatingly and frankly discusses the complex psychic world of the donor—whether for self or as trustee of a major foundation. Wilbur tells us the refreshing truth about both giving *and* getting, and as ever, does it with great respect, compassion, and clear-sightedness. Don't miss it."

—Marilyn Bancel, author of *Preparing Your Capital Campaign*

"Here is a book written with the practical insights and experiential wisdom of leaders who know we are building community one donor, one volunteer, one person in need at a time. Great reading for all of us involved in this work."

—Philip Arca, executive director of St. Vincent de Paul of Alameda County

"Cole Wilbur hits all the right notes in *Giving with Confidence*. The lessons learned from his illustrious career will inspire the new philanthropist while reminding even the most experienced among us to pursue a steady, principled, yet bold approach that will ultimately yield greater impact for the organizations and people we are here to serve. It's a book to keep close to your desk."

—Marc Ross Manashil, cofounder of the Clarence Foundation

"A multifaceted yet clear and simple tool for overcoming the barriers to giving—and to asking. Although aimed at family foundations and individual donors, this book is also a gold mine for grantseekers trying to understand what makes for successful relationships with philanthropists."

—Fred Goff, president emeritus of DataCenter

Giving with Confidence

A Guide to Savvy Philanthropy

Colburn Wilbur
with Fred Setterberg

Heyday, Berkeley, California

Tell me, what is it you plan to do
with your one wild and precious life?
—Mary Oliver, "The Summer Day"

The author and the publisher would like to thank the David and Lucile Packard Foundation for their generous contribution to this project.

Library of Congress Cataloging-in-Publication Data

Wilbur, Colburn S.
    Giving with confidence : a guide to savvy philanthropy / Colburn Wilbur with Fred Setterberg.
        p. cm.
ISBN 978-1-59714-204-5 (hardcover : alk. paper)—
ISBN 978-1-59714-215-1 (apple e-book)—
ISBN 978-1-59714-209-0 (amazon kindle e-book)
    1. Charities. 2. Nonprofit organizations--Management. I. Setterberg, Fred. II. Title.
    HV40.W4895 2012
    361.7′4—dc23   2012008021

Cover Art: Lorraine Rath
Cover and Interior Design/Typesetting: Leigh McLellan Design
Printing and Binding: Thomson-Shore, Dexter, MI

Orders, inquiries, and correspondence should be addressed to:
    Heyday
    P.O. Box 9145, Berkeley, CA 94709
    (510) 549-3564, Fax (510) 549-1889
    www.heydaybooks.com

10 9 8 7 6 5 4 3 2 1

Contents

Acknowledgments

Over the years, our friends and colleagues have contributed to the writing of this book in ways too numerous to mention. We owe them an enormous debt. In particular, we wish to thank:

Ann Van Steenberg	Dawn Hawk	Jonathan London
Anne Ellinger	Dick Letts	Kary Schulman
Art Kuhn	Duncan Beardsley	Kate O'Malley
Barbara Kibbe	Eleanor Friedman	Kathleen Enright
Beth Brown	Elizabeth Wilcox	Ken Nakamura
Bettina Mok	Fred Goff	Kim Bancroft
Bill Somerville	Hugh Burroughs	Kim Klein
Bruce DeBenedictus	Irene Woodward	Krishen Laetsch
Carol Larson	Jan Masaoka	Linda Collins
Carol Van Steenberg	Janet Camerena	Linda Dee
Courtney Martin	Jason Franklin	Lisa Parker
Dan Siegel	Jean Scandlyn	Malcolm Margolin
Dan Suzio	Jeffrey Kessler	Marc Manashil
Dave Peery	Jenny Yancey	Marilyn Bancel

Marjorie Schwarzer

Moira Walsh

Nan Gefen

Nancy Erbstein

Peter Deitz

Philip Arca

Priscilla Macy

Radha Stern

Ralph Lewin

Rick Smith

Ron Rowell

Rushworth Kidder

Sandy Dee

Shirley Fredricks

Susan Orr

Terence Mulligan

Tom Layton

Tracy Gary

William Sterling

Yvonne Rand

and the staff and board of the David and Lucile Packard Foundation.

Introduction

Beyond Flickers

When the subject of philanthropy comes up, I often find myself thinking about lightbulbs.

Lightbulbs?

Let me explain....

During my years as executive director of the David and Lucile Packard Foundation, the lightbulb metaphor frequently surfaced in conversations with Dave Packard.

If your knowledge about a problem is equivalent to a one-watt bulb, Dave used to say—speaking like the engineer that he was—then the area of your illumination will be very small, while the surrounding darkness seems limited. Coming up with an answer is easy because you have no idea what lies out there beyond your tiny flicker of light. You don't know what you don't know.

On the other hand, when your knowledge reaches the equivalent of a 100-watt bulb, you grasp far more, but the amount of darkness surrounding you is also perceived to be much greater. You face complexity, ambiguity, and the unsettling realization that there might not be a single simple solution to your problems.

Now and then, we'd be at a meeting, discussing some social issue or community project, and someone would come up with an approach that would solve all the problems. *If we only did this or tried that, everything would be fine!* Then Dave might tilt his head towards me and whisper, "One-watt bulb…"

Of course, we're all one-watt bulbs on some subjects. But when we're talking about something as multifaceted and important as philanthropy, it's best to state from the outset that none of us has a fully illuminated view of what works best amid a vast and almost limitless universe of funding possibilities.

For that, we have to rely on the accumulated light of our friends, colleagues, mentors, and peers.

Throughout my career, I've learned again and again how much I still have to learn. And after nearly four decades spent working in the foundation world, I'm convinced more than ever that donors who have approached their own philanthropy with imagination, courage, energy, and persistence can point the way towards better giving for us all.

Which is why Fred and I have written this book.

We want to draw upon the example of thoughtful donors and their field-tested techniques to assist:

- individuals giving as little as $5,000 annually,
- families or individual donors giving as much as $500,000 each year, and
- trustees and volunteers in family foundations.

Why mix individual giving with foundation philanthropy? In reality, the majority of our country's 90,000+ foundations are basically family affairs. They operate with assets of $1 million or less. They have no paid professional staff. The responsibility for effective grantmaking sits squarely on the shoulders of the trustees, who face the same dilemmas confronting individual donors: scant time, limited means, and only passing acquaintance with the byways of good giving.

In other words, when it comes to effective philanthropy, we're all groping somewhere in the shadows, if not quite in the dark. We need to turn up our collective wattage to a vast and informative luminosity.

We shouldn't kid ourselves. Good giving is difficult. No less a thinker than Aristotle warned that giving away money is "neither in every man's power nor an easy matter. Hence, it is that such excellence is rare, praiseworthy and noble." Andrew Carnegie, less philosopher than practical man, put it more tartly: "It is more difficult to give money away intelligently than it is to earn it in the first place."

My own experience with philanthropy has been concentrated in the foundation world, a realm rich in opportunities. Foundation executives have access to capital, colleagues, public officials, and leaders in private industry. Sometimes we can even tap the power of the media when we imagine that it will serve our interests. Or we can trundle up to our own private mountaintops and maintain an Olympian silence.

Yet foundations are actually small potatoes when it comes to giving. Individuals deserve the credit for most of our nation's charitable contributions. But since they lack an organizational structure and collective public profile, they're too often ignored in discussions about what makes philanthropy move ahead...

...or veer off course.

This book is written from both sides of the aisle. We're aiming to incorporate some of the best ideas from organized philanthropy *and* individual giving to provide a means for improving the reach, scope, and impact of all our contributions. Nobody has a monopoly on wisdom. We depend on one another.

So what's amiss with philanthropy today? From my perspective, our giving as individuals and small family foundations too often turns out to be:

- **Impulsive** Donors respond to the proverbial (and sometimes literal) knock at the door. That neighborhood canvasser for Greenpeace may make a sound case for saving the world's oceans. But if you really back their program, and you have the means, wouldn't it make more sense to make a larger, more thoughtful gift than the one you're likely to hand over on the spot?

- **Routine** Donors may think hard and long about their first significant contribution to a group, but afterwards, often for years, giving lapses into habit. That's not to say that long-term, few-strings-attached support can't be an excellent strategy. (We'll argue as much in a coming chapter.) But a sustaining commitment differs from an automatic, unexamined gift. Routine can kill the romance in philanthropy. Giving should be electric.

- **Disconnected** Personal relationships are the lifeblood of philanthropy. They're what get us giving in the first place—the pitch from our alma mater, the church pastor, or an old friend testifying on behalf of her favorite cause. But following the first check, the contact between donor and recipient organization often collapses, to the impoverishment of both sides.

- **Overreaching** Some donors grow disenchanted when their initial support fails to eliminate a global scourge such as hunger or poverty. Others misread their contribution as a license to tinker with the organizational gears and pulleys. In both cases, philanthropy suffers. Good giving requires a dose of realism and a light touch.

Instead of succumbing to these four flaws, I want to argue for giving that strives to be:

- Deliberate

- Thoughtful and imaginative

- Connected in all the right places

- Ambitiously realistic

It bears repeating: There isn't any one right way to be an effective donor. Experience teaches us that the methods of good giving are numerous, diverse, and sometimes mutually exclusive. Only the dimmest bulb thinks his way is the only way.

But before we delve into the heart of *how* to give effectively—which makes up the remainder of this book—let's take a moment to explore some of subtle forces governing the psychology and culture of philanthropy.

Giving—and What Gets in Our Way

Giving brings us happiness. The accumulated wisdom of the world's great religions and philosophies tells us so. Our own experience confirms the fact. In terms of quantifiable evidence, we can now turn to laboratory studies showing how generosity recalibrates brain activity and lowers stress levels. Interviews with donors and volunteers reveal them to be happier and healthier than their more tightfisted, disengaged peers. One finding even links giving to increased personal prosperity, with our bank accounts expanding as we donate greater amounts of money and time to causes beyond the welfare of our immediate families.

In sum, giving is good for us. (And not just for the wealthy. America's working poor rank as our nation's most generous people, giving away the greatest percentage of their annual income.) Whatever our material resources, giving can help us wring genuine meaning from mere existence and fill our lives with sustaining, enriching personal relationships.

Then why is it so difficult to do well?

Three factors come immediately to mind.

- **Time** Most of us don't want to turn our giving into a part-time job, particularly when we're dispensing modest amounts.

- **Timing** With kids still in the house, college to pay for, and retirement somewhere around the treacherous bend, the emphasis on philanthropy can feel out of sync with life's rhythms.

- **Uncertainty** Even if we've got the money and the hour seems ripe for a sudden spike of generosity, there's always the nagging question: How do I know my contributions will produce their desired results?

Over the years, I have also come to believe that our instinctual drive towards generosity often gets derailed by more subterranean factors. As donors, we must contend with powerful and largely unconscious fears about:

- **Skepticism** Most individual gifts are very small relative to the needs. In this world of unending trouble and strife, does our pittance really make a difference?

- **Conflict** Not everybody wants to stick out their neck by supporting a controversial cause (which is one reason why Planned Parenthood lists so many of their gifts under the heading "Anonymous").

- **Scandal** The financial misdeeds of a few highly placed officials in prominent national charities have caused too many people to mistake these disgraceful exceptions for the rule (when the real problem in nonprofit life lies in how *little* most staff are paid).

- **Arrogance** "If I'm rich enough to give away my money, then I must be knowledgeable enough to give it away wisely." (See Aristotle and Carnegie.)

- **Mortality** Giving reminds us that our small fortunes may have a longer life than our frail bodies.

- **Embarrassment** Imagine that gnawing feeling in the pit of your stomach as you watch an organization you've supported for years suddenly sink. Now what does that say about *your* judgment?

- **Timidity** Many of the best nonprofits probe society's deepest wounds. Not every donor is willing to bear close witness to this level of deprivation and suffering.

- **Privacy** Philanthropy is a matter of public record. Who wants the limelight shining on their bank account and personal decisions about giving?

- **Fatigue** If you give once, you'll be asked to give again and to give more. Nonprofits must keep asking in order to survive. But for donors, it can feel exhausting, unending, and even disrespectful.

Let's also keep in mind that our motivations for giving are never pure. That may sound jaded, but I prefer to regard this truth as yet another reflection of the human psyche's boundless complexity. Consider the great American philanthropists of the nineteenth century who bequeathed upon posterity all those public libraries, endowed universities, and world-class museums—even as they busted unions, paid off officials, and burnished their reputations as robber barons.

Our own motives may prove no less complex.

- We give in gratitude, to repay the world, in part, for the countless benefits and opportunities we enjoy because of the struggles and sacrifices of those who came before us.

- We give to assuage our consciences—about people suffering on the other side of the world or a few blocks from our homes.

- We give because we're asked by someone we like, admire, or (for complicated reasons we may not like to admit) cannot refuse.

- We give because we want to feel that we're part of the solution, a contributor to society, a person of upstanding character and sound vision.

- We give to get something back—enhanced standing within the community, a reputation for selflessness, richer relationships with other people, or even peace within our family's conflicted factions.

Whether we're aware of it or not, we are usually looking to be rewarded for our giving. Most often, that reward comes in the form of a gratifying emotional experience. Which should be expected. We are social animals. (Aristotle again.) Our contributions of time, talent, and money help sustain us both as individuals and as a civilization.

In the end, the reasons behind our giving may not matter. I suggest we dispense with plunging the psychic depths in favor of recognizing the extraordinary opportunities that presently await us as donors. In truth, the time has never been better to cultivate our skills as individual philanthropists.

Why now?

To begin, there's simply the huge amount of wealth sloshing around our collective checkbooks and brokerage accounts, despite the current downturn. Even in the midst of the worst economic climate in a generation, more than two million Americans still possess investment assets of more than $1 million. And by midcentury, some $40 trillion, according to the most modest estimates, will have traded hands in the greatest intergenerational wealth transfer in history—with higher estimates peaking at $130 trillion. Despite the present difficulties and future perils, we remain a very rich nation with millions of individuals enjoying stable lives of plenty. We can count ourselves among the most fortunate human beings to have inhabited this planet.

Equally important, we need to acknowledge the fact of our own immense freedom. Individual donors enjoy unrivaled independence and autonomy in determining how to use their money for the common good. Unlike business leaders, who must respond to the demands of shareholders, or elected officials, who find themselves bound by tightening budgets and a restive electorate, individual funders and small family foundations are largely responsible only to themselves. As a result, we can move fleetly, conducting our grantmaking with rapid dispatch, jettisoning the stacks of proposals, evaluations, and supplementary materials that too often bog down the foundation world. In light of this independence, our giving should be bolder and less self-interested than anything the business world might attempt—and more imaginative and daring than any program or policy the government is likely to launch.

Finally, we can take comfort in the fact that we now know a great deal about what works and what does not. Decades worth of experimentation, evaluation, revision, and scaling-up success has provided us with a cookbook of strategies for improving education, reducing homelessness, treating drug addiction, and providing working capital to the world's poorest people—to name just a few critically important endeavors. What's more, constantly evolving online technologies are now driving the worldwide promulgation of transformative ideas, best practices, and links between organizations and potential supporters. Donors have never had a wider, richer, and more easily accessed array of funding opportunities to help change the world.

We should revel in these possibilities, even as we embrace the sobering responsibilities engendered by our wealth and freedom.

We should also—dare I say it?—enjoy ourselves. Giving should be gratifying, stimulating, exciting—even fun.

And so in this spirit, we turn now to the experience of intrepid, thoughtful donors who can shed significant light on the many splendors, contradictions, and potentials of good giving.

1

Only Connect

Principle #1 *Follow your connections.*

A colleague in San Francisco recently told me this story:

Her husband came home one evening and mentioned that for some time he had been noticing more and more people living on the edge, barely scraping by. He could see the changes each morning as he walked to his office. More middle-aged men whittling away their days on the corners after passing their nights curled into storefront doorways. More children and mothers among the homeless. A sharper, coarser, meaner feel rising off streets that were already mean enough, and a corresponding dread experienced by the more-fortunate citizens who passed them by each day on their way to work.

He suggested that as a couple they should donate a larger amount this year to basic services—the shelters, food kitchens, and medical teams that allowed some of San Francisco's poorest people to survive. My colleague agreed. Later that week, she wrote out a check to a homeless shelter—located not in San Francisco but across the bay in the smaller, working-class city of Hayward. Instead of contributing three thousand dollars, as she had first planned, she increased the donation to five thousand.

"I was familiar with Hayward," she explained, "because my family had once run a small business there. I knew the shelter and I respected the people running it. I also understood that most people who could afford to contribute a sizeable gift wouldn't be thinking about Hayward, which has the same problems as the big cities but a much smaller pool of donors. And I knew the money was needed now."

In many ways, this donation reflects the best of individual giving. The donors paid attention to the world around them, taking care not to deflect notice of its more painful and distressing aspects. They asked themselves what they could do to make a difference and then took immediate action, waiting neither to be pitched nor publicly praised for their contribution. They relied on their knowledge of local institutions and community needs. And they upped the size of their donation because they grasped that it would make a larger splash in the smaller pond. Their aspirations proved both compassionate and clear eyed: their donation wouldn't eliminate homelessness, but it could provide essential services for some individuals in dire need. In the process, they might also help build an institution in a community that had been largely neglected by big foundations and wealthy donors. Certainly, the contribution had risks attached. Nobody can be absolutely certain how their money will be spent once it leaves their hands. But the risks were informed, calculated, and worth taking—as remains true with any gift worth making.

It's also useful to note what their contribution didn't entail.

Although the couple had donated some forty thousand dollars to various organizations that year, their generosity did not follow the dictates of a formal plan. Despite the encouragement of professional advisors and stacks of recent publications touting the virtues of philanthropy that prides itself on being "strategic," "scientific," "catalytic," or some other adjective yet to burst upon the scene, most donors do no planning whatsoever. Even those who take pride in their familiarity with nonprofit culture and philanthropic methods—even people *employed* by nonprofits and foundations—

usually don't plan their personal donations with the same care they lavish on the purchase of a new computer, automobile, or flat-screen TV. In this, the rich—to reframe F. Scott Fitzgerald's famous assertion—*are* like the rest of us. They may have more money, but they generally do not adhere to any more complicated, demanding, or effective systems for making charitable donations.

Personally, I'm not one to trumpet the cause of time-consuming, paper-laden procedures. I don't chart my own personal contributions with the rigor of a social scientist, and I don't know many people who do. Planning is more typically the province of large philanthropic institutions confront-ing problems of massive scale. If you want to wipe out malaria in Africa, save the world's fisheries, or spark national school reform, then the plan-ning will be copious, professional, and absolutely necessary. But given the relatively small size of individual donations, most donors will rely on other methods.

To begin, they'll pay careful attention to changes they can make close to home.

Pursuing the Personal

Most giving starts with the heart, mind, eyes, and interests of the donor.

We support a local arts organization because as a child we learned to play the trumpet in the school orchestra—and we now deplore a tune-less future bereft of young musicians and audiences unable to distinguish between Brahms, Basie, and the Notorious B.I.G. Or we've watched our own children grow graceful and strong as they absorb a smattering of ballet, salsa, and Indian *bhangra*. Or we attend a concert of teenage performers debuting their own compositions, and we perceive in the heat of the music all the rigor, discipline, and openhearted joy that transforms lives. Or we read a new biography of Louis Armstrong and learn that the happy accident of Satchmo receiving a cornet as a delinquent eleven-year-old boy in New Orleans resulted in him becoming the American Mozart of jazz.

We're touched, altered, inspired, agitated, outraged, filled with hope or dread or longing. And then the spirit moves us to take action.

Certainly the data confirms that most charity begins close to home. A recent tally by Giving USA indicates that the Big Three in philanthropic interests continue to be:

1. **Religion** Congregations and other religious organizations received an estimated $106.89 billion, or 35 percent of total gifts. (Which calls to mind the old fundraising joke: Why do people give so much to churches? Because they ask in person fifty-two times a year!)

2. **Education** Schools, universities, and other teaching organizations received an estimated $40.94 billion, or 13 percent of the total, testifying to the binding power of the old school tie.

3. **Health** Hospitals and related institutions are charted at $21.64 billion, or 7 percent of total estimated giving—a sign of the motivating power of mortality.

In other words, we give first and most prodigiously to organizations that serve our own bodies, minds, and souls—which is understandable and often beneficial.

The question remains: How do we move beyond our personal concerns and our own self-interest to make a broader contribution to the commonweal?

Growing Giving Naturally

"I look for ways to combine my life and my resources," said Nan Gefen. "I came from a family with money, but there was little talk of philanthropy.

The household attitude was, 'Be frugal.' I had to slowly work out for myself what to do with the wealth I inherited over time. Finally, it comes down to learning to trust what you think and what you feel."

As a young woman, Nan "hated" that she had more money than most people she knew. "It felt unreal to me," she said, recalling the jarring contrast between the comfortable home she grew up in and the comparative poverty of many Americans in the 1960s. This disparity prompted her to throw herself into social change movements as an adult, study their rise and fall, and eventually become a psychotherapist. "When I was young, I couldn't see the threads of connection between social and personal life. They seemed to come from separate fabrics. With time, I've learned to tug at those threads and spin new ones wherever I can."

In the mid-1980s, Nan recognized an opportunity to pull together the totality of her emerging personal interests—philanthropic, political, and sacred—with the founding of *Tikkun*, a magazine for "spiritual progressives" based on the Hebraic injunction to "heal, repair, and transform the world." She was a "co-collaborator" on the magazine's conception and promotion, worked as the publisher, and contributed essential funding for the first six years. Drawn by the religion's values, she also converted to Judaism, finding for herself a new spiritual home. "I felt compelled to become a Jew," she recalled, noting how her life and her philanthropy were starting to "merge."

One decisive step leads to another. By the 1990s, Nan was prompted by the "growing centrality of Jewish spiritual practice in [her] life" to help found another institution—Chochmat HaLev, a community center for prayer, study, celebration, and meditation "in an atmosphere that is friendly, warm, authentic, and meaningful." ("This is not your parents' synagogue," proclaims the website.) Once again, Nan's financial contributions—key to the center's being able to buy a building—were matched by significant gifts of time and talent. She taught courses on mysticism, spiritual practice, and meditation, and helped the governing board plan for the future. "I needed to establish myself as a teacher and community member."

Experience also taught Nan the value of establishing the limits of her financial assistance. "It's important to know as a donor when to pull back," she observed. "I made it clear that I'd diminish my giving over time so there was room for others to step forward. And they did." After the cofounding Rabbi left, she remained active in the organization's governance until a successor could be hired. "I felt good about staying on through the center's birth pangs and into a new stage. In a way, I was protecting my investment."

In the best spirit of conscious, connected giving, Nan allowed her personal interests to blossom into public benefit. She got involved—deeply, wholeheartedly, persistently. Her money was critical to each endeavor, but her time, skills, and commitment proved equally important.

Most recently, Nan has started *Persimmon Tree*, an online magazine of the arts featuring the writing, poetry, and art of women over sixty. "I've learned," she said, "that I have a gift for breathing life into a project, and helping it to move beyond its infancy. Having money has enabled me to do some very creative work for a number of years and I really don't see it coming to an end. I'm going to turn seventy in a few weeks, and I'm thinking: *What do I want to do now?*"

In Praise of Planning

The paucity of planning for charitable donations was recently illustrated in a 2010 report conducted by HOPE Consulting. The Money for Good initiative surveyed individuals with household incomes over $80,000, a group that represents the nation's top third in terms of wealth and makes 75 percent of all individual contributions. While 85 percent of respondents stated that the performance of a donor group was "very important" to them, only 35 percent indicated that they conduct research on any gift. As far as those who sit down with family members to hammer out a lifetime or even annual giving plan—well, we don't have the data, but all accounts suggest that it's an exceedingly slender slice of the funding pie.

Which is not to say that we don't *need* to plan. Thoughtful planning would almost certainly improve American philanthropy in several ways.

First, we would be shielded from impulsive giving unrelated to our core values and vision of change. We'd be less disposed to silver-tongued promoters, gimmicky trends, and our own worst instincts. We'd resist the temptation to engage in rescue funding—an almost hopeless, if overindulged, practice whereby donors stuff dollars into the hull of some sinking nonprofit, hoping to fill in the gaps and piece together a few more years of rickety use.

Planning also increases the likelihood of giving more money over time. Deliberation breeds commitment. Once we know what we want to accomplish, we're more likely to drive full-steam ahead. Conversely, it's hard to work up enthusiasm about flailing around in the dark.

Most important, planning strengthens our inclination and ability to grapple with complicated, challenging goals and then prod them into existence over a number of years. Plans can serve as a map, blueprint, and reminder note about where we're going and why. The planning process—far more important than the plan itself—shakes up our thinking about what's possible and then bolsters our intellect, imagination, and ethical clarity to get the job done.

But if planning is so good for us, why do we resist it?

- **Lack of role models** Experienced philanthropists accurately observe that much of the grantmaking practiced by their peers remains unapologetically plan-less—including efforts in a large swath of the foundation world. Few of us have witnessed our friends and colleagues construct a personal life giving plan. We don't know what they look like or how to create them. We haven't seen them put to excellent use.

- **Discomfort and uncertainty** A frank conversation about the world we want to leave behind can challenge our musty old ideas about philanthropy. Or more likely, it will point to even wispier and more inchoate notions about somehow doing some good somewhere someday. It may even underscore family conflicts, since we're apt to collide with our spouses, children, and our own divided selves as we strain to prioritize life goals and related gifts.

- **Time and cost** Planning takes time, and few of us feel that we possess enough of this precious commodity. After a few false starts, we may conclude that we need to hire a wealth advisor or planning consultant. But that comes with its own price tag (despite the fact that a skilled professional may in the end save both time and money).

- **Past experience** If you've spent your career in business, government, or academia, you already may have had your fill of endless meetings devoted to planning processes run amok. Or you may recall excellent plans crafted over many hours that were finally abandoned before the implementation got started. You may be understandably reluctant to get anywhere near another plan.

- **Overwhelmed by accountability** If you don't know where you want to go and how to get there, you can't be blamed by anybody, including yourself, for failing to arrive. The fact that our reluctance to accept personal responsibility for giving remains largely unconscious makes it all the more powerful.

- **Lack of outside pressure** Nobody will complain if you don't plan your charitable giving. Nobody will ever know. If a plan is in your philanthropic future, you'll be the one who makes it happen.

Fortunately, today's reluctant planner can rely on several useful tools developed in recent years. For a series of helpful exercises devoted to

Five Questions to Ask Yourself before You Give

1. Am I really interested in this organization? Sure, it's a good group doing important work. But does it touch *you*? Are you intrigued by its mission, its programs, perhaps even its swagger and style? Is there enough happening between the two of you to keep the relationship percolating for a decent interval? Or are you likely to lose interest and wander away?

2. What changes do I want to see in the world over the next five years? The next ten—or thirty? Time to daydream. You're looking for an orientation—goals that may not be obtainable in your lifetime but nevertheless seem worth aiming for. Even though nobody's going to hold you to your answers, it's still crucial to ask the big questions.

3. What would I regret failing to do now if I don't give it a try? Think about that project you've been itching to launch but as yet haven't—that problem, absence, or injustice that still makes your blood boil. Now do something about it.

4. Who are my heroes? We're talking about the people engaged in society's important work. For you, they may be agronomists laboring south of the Sahara, a troupe of actors staging *Romeo and Juliet* in the park, or community organizers riling things up in your own downtown. Now go out and meet them.

5. What kind of giving sounds fun? Philanthropy shouldn't be grim and dutiful. After all, the word means "love of humankind." If you're going to stick with conscious giving for the long haul, you'll need to enjoy yourself. Try to imagine what might start your philanthropic chops salivating.

imagining a better world and your philanthropic plans to hasten its coming, consult *Inspired Philanthropy: Your Step-By-Step Guide to Creating a Giving Plan* by Tracy Gary and Melissa Kohner, part of the Chardon Press Series published by Jossey-Bass. Or pick up a copy of *The Generosity Plan: Sharing Your Time, Treasure, and Talent to Shape the World* by Kathy LeMay. Both books make excellent guides.

Extending Your Reach

I'm a lucky man. For nearly four decades, I've had the privilege to work with smart, imaginative, ambitious people dedicated to making our world more just, beautiful, bountiful, and sustainable. As a foundation executive and individual donor, I've been able to watch and sometimes pitch in during critical battles to save the wilderness, protect the oceans' health, and lighten our international energy footprint. My colleagues and I have helped direct funds to underwrite public school music programs, advance basic research in science and engineering, and build the world-class Monterey Bay Aquarium.

In short, I can't think of a better way to have spent my professional life.

But I also know that many of the tools I have relied on throughout my foundation career don't work for most individual donors.

Individuals, along with smaller family foundations, lack the time, experience, infrastructure, and staffing to:

- immerse themselves in complex research,

- construct and analyze detailed plans,

- negotiate among competing interests,

- scale up fledgling efforts to meet national and international demands, and

- conduct rigorous evaluations, perhaps years after the first grants have been dispatched.

Individual donors require a different approach to connect them wisely, viscerally, and creatively to their nonprofit partners.

Their first step should be to toss out the formal apparatus of foundation grantmaking.

That's right—dispense with the grant proposal as the primary, and all-too-often sole, evidence of nonprofit capability. Or at least give yourself a protracted break from endless reading so that you can take advantage of the individual donor's autonomy and freedom out in the real world.

Here's why I'm skeptical about some grant applications: Organized philanthropy's elaborate procedures often result in nothing more than a time-devouring burden for both sides. Consider the countless hours—surely, in the millions each year—devoted to pounding out grant applications that will come to naught. Imagine the days, weeks, and months wasted over their perusal and almost-inevitable rejection. Grantmaking generates too much paper with too few results. In the foundation world, justifiable reasons may exist for the winding paper trail of grant review and approval (though not nearly enough reason for the volume produced and the hours wasted). But as individual donors, we have no excuse. We're free. We can slough off the paper shackles.

What should you be doing if not reviewing mounting heaps of deadly-dull grant applications?

You should get out in the world and meet the people undertaking its important work.

Good people are the key to every successful voluntary effort. Success doesn't just blossom from the seed of excellent design. Rather, it's powered by *people* capable of transforming plans into reality. Lots of nonprofit professionals can write good grant proposals. (Some can even render them into highly imaginative works of art.) But grant proposals are to programs what marriage proposals are to marriages. The success of both are entirely dependent on the people involved—hopefully, over the long run.

Here's what I look for in nonprofit leaders:

- **Blazing ambition** They're fired by a passion to make the world a better place.

- **Keen vision** They see a way to turn their ambitions into effective action.

- **Open ears** They know how to listen to everybody at the table and they use what they learn to improve their organization's performance.

- **Dependable instincts** They exhibit a felt sense about what works and what doesn't, who's reliable and who isn't.

- **Utter determination** They're in the game for the long haul, undeterred by inevitable setbacks, inspired by occasional victories.

- **Modesty and humor** They can laugh about almost anything— including themselves.

How to Meet the Best People: The Art of Site Visits

How do you locate outstanding leaders within the nonprofit field?

One of the best ways is to visit organizations on their own turf.

Over the years, I've conducted countless site visits with organizations large and small. If I have one regret in my career, it's probably that I didn't spend more time talking directly with the nonprofit leaders our foundation supported. It's really the most engaging part of the job, the time when your assumptions get challenged and you learn about a variety of issues with a depth and specificity that can't be duplicated from the far-flung distance of your desk.

Now, I can hear somebody saying, "That's fine for a foundation person, but how can I just drop by an organization and ask questions? They'll think I'm weird, or wasting their time, or getting ready to write them a check."

The trick is to counter all of those (mis)perceptions with blatant honesty.

It starts with a phone call. You contact the individual in charge and explain your interests. *Yes, you've supported a number of nonprofit efforts in the past, but for the moment, you're simply interested in learning more. Could you have an hour of the organization's time?*

Of course, you do your homework. You've read the website, talked with anybody you might know who's had direct experience with the organization. You've got a provisional vision of the organization—a working theory ready to be altered by experience. You write down a few questions to clarify some points. Basically, they come down to four areas of inquiry—with tentacles…

- What's working? How do you know your group is having an effect? How do you measure progress? What's the quantifiable evidence? What does your gut tell you that you would never read in a formal proposal? How would the group use a modest-sized grant to make a difference?

- What's uncertain? Is there information you desire that you don't yet have? Where are the holes in your understanding? Why do they exist? What can you do to fill them?

- What keeps people working here? What motivates the executive and staff? What are the biggest problems they face? How do they deal with them on a daily basis?

- What does the future look like? How will you know that you've achieved your mission? What's your timetable for success? What are your most vulnerable points? How long does the director intend to stick with the job? Are there plans for succession? Does the board and staff have a plan for where the organization should be three years from now?

Mind your tone. You're not an investigative journalist, grand inquisitor, or organizational consultant ready to ladle on the unsolicited advice. Neither are you (yet) a committed ally. In a word, you're *interested*. A better word: you're there to *learn*.

Even if you have the deftest touch, you'll still be negotiating a tricky power dynamic. The group needs money. You've got some. Your very presence tenders delectable possibilities. Don't be coy, but nevertheless try not to raise unrealistic expectations.

Repeat as necessary: *I'm just here to find out a little more about your work…*

Limit your visit to no more than an hour or two. (Nobody's going to ask you to leave. It's up to you to behave like a good guest and vacate accordingly.) Also keep in mind: Staff may defer to your advice, even when it's lousy. Be sparing with suggestions. Have I mentioned that you're there to listen?

Also be aware that your presence may have unintended effects on program participants.

"I wish donors were more educated about issues of class and culture," the director of a nonprofit working with low-income teens said frankly. "They don't always realize that our kids feel awkward telling their personal stories, particularly if they end up doing it repeatedly for a procession of donors. I'd like visitors to talk with our staff and find out what kinds of questions are off-limits and learn to recognize what our kids may be feeling. It'd be great if they'd explain to the kids who they are, where their money came from, and why they're trying to give it away. In a perfect world, they'd show interest in our kids as human beings, not social problems. And they'd give them an insight into what makes philanthropy tick and how a responsible person of means behaves."

Making Connections Count

Only connect. That's the epigraph to *Howards End,* E. M. Forster's 1910 novel about the conflicts of class and culture, and the kind of society that may evolve from individuals reaching beyond their conventional boundaries. One hundred years later, Forster's command still resonates. Far more than our adherence to principles and abstractions, we're called to action—including philanthropy—by our experience and emotions: the heart of our connections to others. How do we ensure that these connections prove fruitful?

Over the years, I've observed that effectively connected donors adhere to four basic principles.

1. Know thyself.

A successful philanthropist knows what he cares about, what quickens his pulse, what lies in the corner of his darkest fears. Of course, there is no right or final answer. The task is to repeatedly ponder: What kind of society do I want to build? What are the problems I feel suited to battle? What achievements of the past might I *now* improve upon? Life as a conscious donor presents an unending opportunity—no, let's make that *obligation*—to better understand yourself even as you're learning more about the world. Do I feel a visceral tug when I'm in the company of children—or animals? Am I moved most deeply by the possibilities of life when I'm trekking along a silent mountaintop, or listening to the culminating strains of Verdi's *Requiem*—or better yet, singing in the chorus?

You can pick up any number of tools to help clarify your philanthropic aspirations. Try writing a frank letter to your grandchildren (even if they're yet to be born) about the kind of world you hope they will inherit and what you fear may stand in their way. Don't send the letter to anybody, but read it over now and then as an honest testament to your better, braver nature. Or take an hour's walk in undistracted silence and allow yourself to really *feel* the fears and aspirations you harbor for your family, your town, the country, the world. Or invite two close friends to dinner for the sole purpose of discussing what you all hope your personal giving will accomplish. Don't talk about the organizations you plan to support but rather the kinds of changes you want to hasten. Dwell in the dreamland of what's possible, what's necessary, what you most fervently desire. Object when any of you resorts to bombast, false sentiment, or any other rhetorical feint that moves your conversation away from the heartfelt and raw.

Remember, too, that we are all creatures of our common culture and our particular subcultures, each with our own set of preferences, biases, and judgments. We must be attentive to our complex backgrounds, recognizing that they provide us with both sources of insight and blind spots. The alert donor strives to remain aware of all he doesn't know and cannot easily perceive when endeavoring to work outside his own community.

On a more mundane level, consult your checkbook and tax records to find out where your donations have actually gone in the past year or two. Fill a page with the amount of each gift and the name of the corresponding organization. Ask yourself: Given what I have, have I given enough? Do my donations jibe with my ambitions? Are there glaring holes in my giving patterns—or are there opportunities shining through?

Allow yourself to dream, trust your instincts, try to be braver than you really think you are.

2. Get involved beyond giving.

Money shields us from discomfort, danger, and disagreeable truths. It's a kind of insulation. It can also throw up barriers and blind us to our potential to join in the vital, unsung labor of remaking the world. If an organization is worth sending a check, it should also be worthy of your time and effort, your own sweat equity.

At the Packard Foundation, we urge our trustees to volunteer with the groups we fund. Oftentimes, this involvement grows into a long-term commitment. I've served as a trustee at Colorado College in Colorado Springs, where David Packard's parents attended school. It's a connection I'd never have made without the nudge, and it's also one I intend to maintain as long as I'm needed.

"Donors should work both sides of the philanthropic street," advised an active giver. "They should get involved in the nonprofit sector and learn what it's like to be looking for money as well as giving it away. I've done that for years, and it's given me greater understanding of the field, more respect for the people doing the asking, and a very informed and critical eye for the roles we're all playing."

3. Know your limits and chart an exit strategy.

You can't help everybody. Choices must be made. Thoughtful ones. That's what's meant by prioritizing: Given the limits of your money, time, interests, and energy, where should you begin?

Aim for connections you can stick with for several years. A fickle donor can be worse than no donor at all if erratic support raises expectations and then dashes them.

Of course, none of us are needed forever. Nor do we usually want our commitments to be perceived as unending. That's why you should construct an exit plan at the beginning of your relationship. You'll feel a bit freer knowing that you're not committed in perpetuity, and the organization will have fair warning about when they should begin preparing for your departure. In some cases, your exit strategy may be "never." You may plan to stick it out to the end of your days (or beyond, if you've been conscientious about your legacy gifts). Whatever your intentions, it's important to surface them early in frank conversation with the group's leadership.

4. Think in terms of partnership.

Some donors can be a nuisance. Their financial support may be limited, but they prove unstinting in their advice and criticism of staff. They advocate for pet projects that require organizational undergirding and they ceaselessly demand attention *right now!* Your contribution, however important, doesn't make you a member of the starting team. You're a fan and booster. Your donation will require staff time to record and manage. Don't add more than a couple of hours to the burden. The staff and board should express their gratitude, write a nice thank you, and perhaps try to cultivate an even bigger pledge next year. (Like it or not, that's their responsibility. A good development team is ceaselessly pitching.) A good funding partner remains aware of the costs that his contributions entail for the staff. He knows how to make suggestions with a delicate touch and, more important, when to back off.

Instead of vocalizing about programs and policies, try asking the organization's leaders what kind of assistance *they* need. That might include a fresh eye on old problems. Or sparkling language about the group's long-standing virtues. (If you can articulate why you support the organization, you may supply the words and rationale for other donors—and in terms that would otherwise remain elusive to staff.) Or perhaps the best contribution is silence.

Think of yourself as an emissary for the organization you support as you travel through your own social and professional spheres. Encourage friends and colleagues to donate. Volunteer to accompany the executive director or development staff on fundraising visits. You will find that you can be extraordinarily persuasive because of your own demonstrable commitment.

"One of the most important things I've done," one donor said, "is making connections between organizations. I've been proud to be a roving ambassador for nonprofits that should have known each other but didn't— and then end up working together after I bring them together." Keep an eye open for the unexpected ally with whom you may have entrée—the city manager, a potential donor, the leaders of another excellent nonprofit whose symmetry with your own cause has yet to be perceived. Be sure to float the prospective introduction past your group's director before taking any steps.

Even More Personal: Giving to Individuals

Most philanthropy goes directly to nonprofit organizations. But sometimes we may feel the call to aid an individual. As far as the tax implications go—well, best to consult your accountant. They can be complex. Just be aware that the concept of "charitable purposes" is sufficiently elastic to include an individual in need or somebody undertaking important work outside the shelter of 501(c)(3) nonprofit status. Whatever the complications—and there are usually fewer legal ones than most people fear—you may stumble upon an opportunity that is simply too promising to ignore.

That was certainly the case at the Packard Foundation when we began our fellowship program for young scientists and engineers. Dave Packard came up with the idea. He wanted to encourage researchers during the first three years of their university tenure track, a time when financial support can be difficult to obtain. Our program identified energetic, creative minds and then provided them with the financial means to advance their work and remain in the field. We kept the funds flexible. If a scientist discovered that his initial line of inquiry wasn't producing results, he could make a sharp turn and try something else. That's not the usual procedure in most institutions given the rigid strictures of government grants. But we trusted our fellows and they have consistently rewarded our confidence.

Our experience with the Packard Fellows convinces me that philanthropy has much more room for support of individuals in a variety of unconventional circumstances. A handful of fellowships provide support directly to individuals without any institutional infrastructure. The MacArthur "Genius Awards" operate in this fashion, as do the National

Endowment for the Arts fellowships for prose writers, poets, and translators. To my mind, we would benefit as a society with more no-strings fellowships awarded to creative artists, scientists, and thinkers outside the academy.

One of the benefits of giving to an individual is the prospect for immediate impact. Unlike donations pooled in the coffers of a large organization whose remote beneficiaries will forever remain invisible, aid to an individual may reap results you can see. By stepping in where others fear to tread, you may spark changes in the life of one person—or the effort she leads—that will ripple down through the years.

Yet proximity can also bring discomfort. You can't cloak yourself in anonymity. The encounter may prove intimidating, even embarrassing. You're involved, there's no getting around it, and the product of your intervention, or its lack, is joyously or excruciatingly apparent. Working closely with an individual, you may also experience more emotion than you've bargained for—distress, disappointment, even heartbreak, as well as the elation of success. It's a hotter, more passionate, riskier kind of giving. The gratifications can be great, but so are the chances of error.

Take, for example, this tale of two gifts…

Although Sarah had been raised in a wealthy family, she supported herself as a high school teacher, working for decades in poor communities and devoting hours after school to her students' academic and personal struggles. Oftentimes, her students remained close following graduation, embracing Sarah as their mentor while they strove to find work or enter college. One afternoon, Sarah met with several former students at a local café and noticed that Zack, one of her favorites from a few years before, couldn't seem to follow the conversation. He confessed that his hearing had declined to the point of near-deafness since his operation for a brain tumor in twelfth grade. The hearing loss proved particularly frustrating because Zack was now working in a youth center, and longed to continue, but found that he could no longer make sense out of the din of conversation, shouts, and squabbles. A hearing aid was out of the question: $3,000—far beyond his family's ability to help out. Zack had never known anybody with this amount of ready cash that wasn't already spoken for several times over.

Sarah went home that night, wrote a check for the full amount, and mailed it to him. "It was a big chunk of money focused on a solid outcome," she recalled. "By extension, I figured that I was helping to launch a career serving kids that was being undertaken by a young person who had suffered himself." Zack called Sarah as soon as he received the check. "He was crying; he couldn't believe it. I just said, 'Take it. Use it.' I didn't think about following up. Once I give money, it's out there—it's no longer mine. I trust it's going to work out somehow."

Except when it doesn't. Not long after underwriting Zack's hearing aid, Sarah spoke with another former student whose life had taken a decidedly downward turn. After high school, she got pregnant, moved into the projects to raise her son alone, and worked sporadically. One barrier to a steady job was her car—"a heap of smoking junk," recalled Sarah. Since Sarah was buying a new car, and had only been offered one hundred dollars trade-in for her older model, she gave it to her student, who duly promised to fix the brakes and switch over the registration. And that, figured Sarah, was that. A nice bit of resource reallocation, a tool placed in the hands of somebody who needed it and now had an opportunity to use it well.

"But she didn't change the pink slip," said Sarah. "I know because five months later, I got a call from a police detective in Las Vegas asking about the car. It had been found in an empty lot with two young men in the back seat shot dead." The car had made its way from Sarah's hands to her student to somebody else who committed the murders. Sarah had to fly to Nevada to testify about the little she knew. Somewhere along the way, the unassailable common sense of the gift had collapsed.

"My student and I both came from alcoholic moms," said Sarah, recalling what she now saw as her overidentification with the young woman.

"But my dad was wealthy and he could send us to private school and step into the fray if we got in trouble. We had all kinds of resources. My student didn't have anybody who could move her beyond her upbringing. I wanted to be that person. But I couldn't. Not at that point—maybe never. You have to be very clear about who you're giving the money to, and what for. It's complicated—which doesn't mean I wouldn't do something similar again. But I always look closely and try to anticipate what might be coming down the road."

It's easy to make mistakes when giving to an organization or an individual. You can waste money and time, and end up paralyzed by your own disappointment. But despite all the talk about "due diligence," most foundation grantmakers go no further than Sarah did in guaranteeing the good use of their dollars. In truth, the personal connection she established with her students brought her much closer to perceiving the possibilities and liabilities of each gift.

Sometimes individual grantmaking turns out well; other times, it doesn't. Your judgment and ability to distinguish between genuine opportunities, wishful thinking, and straight-out con games will make an enormous difference to the success rate. Like all grantmaking—like all complex and ambitious human endeavors—you can't always win. But to assume from the start that the task is too daunting to try is to rob yourself of the potential for doing a great deal of good.

Too Close for Comfort: When Connections Get Complicated

Active donors may eventually feel that they're being taken advantage of. It's unfortunate and regrettable. It may also be inevitable. To some eyes, you will always be a walking dollar sign. It can hurt your feelings.

Or worse.

I'm thinking right now about a seasoned donor who spoke about her experience accompanying an executive director on a fundraising visit to a person the ED tellingly referred to only as their "prospect." The woman's husband had just died and the executive kept directing the conversation back to his memory, deliberately churning the widow's grief. Then he pounced. *Now, I know your husband would want to help us out, if only he was here....*

"It turned my stomach," said the donor. "It was shocking. But there I was—stuck in the middle. On some level, it happens all the time. A person comes along with money, and they become 'other'—not quite human."

What can you do about it?

Not much. It's probably hopeless trying to persuade someone to see you as a full-fledged human if they're determined to fixate on your bank account.

Finally, we must learn to live with the contradictions inherent to our role as funders. Philanthropy is work. No matter how rewarding the results, no matter how heartening the human connections, our efforts to improve the world remain a struggle. The fact that the full dimensions of our individual humanity may not always be recognized isn't the main point.

Still, if we listen to philanthropists who have maintained their commitments for many years, perhaps we can gain some perspective.

Recently, a donor who has contributed thousands of hours in volunteer time, as well as considerable cash donations, put into words his own formula for reconciling his aspirations with the unavoidable disappointments.

"In order to have a good experience," he said, "I have to see that I'm not operating in a vacuum. I want to feel some camaraderie—or, at least, know that the people I'm working with are paying attention. Sometimes, it doesn't happen. Nobody even says thanks." He shrugged his shoulders. "Next time, perhaps, I'll make a different decision and work with somebody who does. But I keep working because my experience tells me that there are plenty of good partners out there. I just haven't met them all yet."

2

Extending Your Reach

Principle #2 *Send your money where you can't go.*

"A dozen years ago," recalled Susan Orr, "I suddenly realized that most of my giving was going to people like me."

For decades, Susan had generously underwritten her alma mater, backed environmental organizations and parks, responded frequently to needs within her local community and beyond.

"I even traveled to Rwanda," she recalled. "I saw the mountain gorillas and met with the conservationists trying to protect them. Are mountain gorillas the most pressing issue in the world? Probably not." But Susan's experience in Africa moved her. Moreover, she personally knew the researcher heading up the fieldwork. It was another case of weighing in alongside individuals from her own demographic: well-educated, affluent professionals, keen on using science and technology to halt environmental degradation and alleviate human suffering. Good work—without a doubt. But she felt that something was missing.

"The big question for me," insisted Susan, "was how to give to people *unlike* myself who really needed it. I wanted to reach the poorest of the poor—people I wouldn't meet under ordinary circumstances."

Susan recognized the difficulties inherent to her ambition. The conditions of poverty constitute a world of its own—complex, multifarious, too distant from the experience of most wealthy donors to be apprehended with clarity. She refused to deceive herself into thinking that she could master this beguiling context overnight. Nor did she want to make wasteful mistakes.

So she asked Bill Somerville, President of Philanthropic Ventures Foundation, to keep his eyes open for funding opportunities within the Bay Area's poorest communities.

Now, Bill Somerville is an extraordinary person. As a foundation executive, he's spent most of his career directing money towards grassroots leaders in marginalized communities. He shuns meetings, proposal reading, and professional associations in order to spend the maximum amount of time out in the field where he can locate exceptional individuals who might otherwise escape the notice of conventional funders. He's brash, opinionated, fearless, highly skilled, and absolutely sincere. He's also been a close friend of mine for many years. I knew that Susan's brave and unusual choice made perfect sense.

"If I wrote down what I value most in terms of good work," confided Susan, "you'd see an emphasis on helping the most impoverished communities in this country, and aiding poor women everywhere. In each case, they are hard to reach. When I review my giving, I can see that although I'm quite clear about my preferences, the bulk of my money doesn't go to these ends. That's where Bill came in."

Following Susan's request, Bill returned quickly with recommendations for her giving. Not that he had to do anything out of the ordinary. During the course of his work, Bill frequently encountered projects that met the criteria of reaching "the poorest of the poor." Sometimes, the money required proved modest. Fifteen hundred dollars for brown-bag lunches to feed one hundred hungry people in a downtown center on Sundays. Five hundred dollars for paints, brushes, and paper to be used in a free work-shop for low-income kids who otherwise might never get involved in the arts. Other times, he pointed Susan towards more substantial endeavors that promised significant impact and an enduring ripple of salutary effects. One grant helped immigrant mothers learn English. Their studies led to steady employment in their children's public schools, where they helped connect Spanish-speaking families with the classroom teachers. As a result, students improved their attendance and earned higher grades, while parents participated more frequently and thoroughly in classroom activities. Another grant underwriting a school for immigrant youth proved so successful that a major funder stepped in, freeing Susan's funds for new projects. With each grant, trust grew stronger between Susan and Bill. Soon, she was relying implicitly on his judgment, enabling him to make grants swiftly, sometimes even on the spot.

Learning About Places You'll Never Go

The use of an intermediary, like Bill Somerville, can lead you to individuals and organizations that would otherwise remain invisible. Nobody in the world is so well connected that they can't benefit from an additional pair of eyes and ears—not to mention feet traveling to places you might never venture. But it's also a high-trust proposition requiring thoughtful preparation.

"In my town, there are plenty of neighborhoods I know nothing about," said one donor who has frequently relied on community members to turn up funding opportunities. "I don't speak the language, I don't know the community leaders, I'm only vaguely aware of the problems and know nothing about the opportunities. Maybe I've never even walked these streets. I look for somebody who can compensate for my deficits."

What kind of person makes a trustworthy intermediary? Likely candidates will:

- know the culture, language, and major players in the community you want to help,

- continue to listen to and learn from people who don't usually meet with donors or representatives from organized philanthropy,

- have a strong desire to lend a hand—but never a vested interest in supporting any particular organization,

- possess personal values and a social consciousness consonant with your own philanthropic orientation,

- be well versed in the fields that interest you, and

- enjoy sufficient initiative and courage to poke around in places where you might find yourself overwhelmed, confused, conflicted, frightened, or otherwise ill suited to look for yourself.

Capable people tend to know one another. Your best bet in finding a reliable partner is to first consult individuals you already know and trust. Ask the people you admire to point you towards candidates well suited by temperament and experience to serve as scouts for projects that might warrant further investigation. The individuals who get recommended may surprise you. In many poor neighborhoods, the people with an ear to the ground aren't necessarily the credentialed social service providers, elected officials, or reputed leaders whose names turn up repeatedly in the news. Rather, you may get your best leads from the single mother in a tough district who has opened her home to children needing a safe place to play after school. Or the former Golden Gloves competitor who's running a makeshift gym out of his garage. Or the church deacon who has taken it upon himself to make certain that his congregation's poorest people get fed at the end of Sunday services. You may need to set aside your longstanding assumptions about where expertise comes from and who is qualified to make judgments about community assets and social capital. But with a bit of trust and daring, you can form a working relationship with individuals from any number of backgrounds who have devoted their lives to bringing to light the best in places where too often only the worst gets noticed.

Keep in mind the following principles:

1. Seek experience, expertise, and genuine interest. When Bill Somerville began working with Susan Orr, he was already scouring the five counties surrounding his office for promising projects and capable leaders. Indeed, this effort was central to his professional aims and personal mission.

2. Recruit outside of your usual realm of acquaintance. Your partner should lift you out of the groove of philanthropic routine. In fact, you may get your best tips from journalists (who prize themselves on being in the know). Or juvenile court judges and probation workers (who see critical needs going unmet every day). Or small business owners, community board volunteers, high school counselors.

3. Clarify your own expectations. From the beginning, be explicit about your goals. Outline the work you expect to see accomplished. Plainly state your intermediary's hours and compensation. For instance: *I want to help teenagers in the San Antonio district stay in school until they graduate. I'd like you to spend ten hours (or twenty, or one hundred…) talking with people in the district, making site visits, nosing around in places I couldn't begin to find or feel comfortable investigating on my own. In two months, I want you to come back with three recommendations for funding (or the names of five groups I should visit on my own, or the single most productive project, organization, or person working in this field). For this assignment, I'll pay you—*

Community Foundations as Intermediaries

A skilled and motivated intermediary can be a great boon for individual donors or small family foundations lacking staff or volunteers to handle the prodigious legwork that good philanthropy demands.

But what if you can't find the right person? Or you don't have enough time to conduct a careful search? Or you're simply uneasy about delegating responsibility to somebody who may at least start out as a stranger?

Surely, there's a simpler solution?

An obvious choice does exist for donors seeking expert advice on local funding opportunities. Donors can turn to their local community foundation. At least, in theory. Practice, as we shall see, can be a more complicated matter.

But first, a few words about why community foundations exist and how they function…

Community foundations draw together the collective resources of many donors to serve the needs of a limited geographic region—usually a city or discrete segment of a large state. Governed by a diverse board of community representatives, rather than the family members or corporate officers who dominate private and corporate foundations, the community foundation relies on paid professional staff to analyze local needs and construct strategies for meeting them.

The last two decades have been boom years for community foundations. In 1987, only one hundred institutions operated nationally. Today, the number stands well above eight hundred. During my tenure at the Packard Foundation, we worked with a number of California community foundations to help build their capacities to both identify local needs and galvanize funders—all in the service of creating a durable locus of philanthropic expertise and action. Other large foundations throughout the country have assumed responsibility for seeding and staffing start-up institutions in their states' rural counties. Not so long ago, it seemed as though most of the country would soon be able to boast its own home-grown funder.

Community foundations offer loads of benefits. By aggregating the limited resources of many donors, they can tackle substantive problems too daunting for individuals to consider. Staff can immerse themselves in the local nonprofit culture and provide knowledgeable funding recommendations to both individual donors and the board that determines the course of discretionary monies. The foundation can launch initiatives and link arms with like-minded funders on a large scale. Donors have the opportunity to gather together to hone their philanthropic skills, learn from one another, and pool their ambitions and experience as well as their funds.

Anyway, that's the ideal. But on the way to building a national infrastructure of community foundations, I'm sorry to report that the communal impulse has frequently dwindled to a throb. Today, most community foundations serve largely as receptacles for donor-advised funds. Driven by professional advisors and the financial services industry, this flexible, no-fuss model of giving enables wealthy individuals to assign their money to a separate account, indicate their funding preferences, and delegate to staff the check writing, accounting, and related paperwork. In increasing num-·bers of community foundations, that's now what staff *mostly* do. According to an analysis by the National Philanthropic Trust, the donor-advised fund now ranks as the nation's fastest-growing tool for charitable giving, with more than 122,500 funds in existence in 2008—and a combined worth of $27.7 billion that has doubled over a mere five years. Now, there's certainly an important role to be played by donor-advised funds. At a minimum, they prove attractive to new donors, bringing to philanthropy great caches of wealth. But as the donor-advised fund gains an ever-stronger hold on community foundations, the promise of collective enterprise shepherded by a knowledgeable staff and board is beginning to recede into the distance.

"In my program," said one former staffer at a large community foundation, "I had perhaps five people I could count on to work together on larger projects that the foundation had identified as important. Five out of five hundred funds. When we surveyed the donors, most said that they didn't want to be contacted by us or have suggestions brought forward for funding."

Community foundations now find themselves in a quandary. They want to grow their assets and serve the community. But they face stiff competition from the financial services industry, which offers the same accounting assistance at a lower cost. What community foundations can offer that businesses can't is a thorough knowledge of funding opportunities. But if the staff is occupied most of the time with servicing donor-advised funds, instead of wading out into the community to meet people, learn, and grow more knowledgeable with time, then they're surrendering their natural advantage.

"If I knew where I wanted my money to go," admitted a former consultant to community foundations, "I'd probably use one of the financial services firms myself, since they can do it cheaper. Or I'd give directly to the organization and bypass the middleman altogether. I'd only go to a community foundation if I was certain they really had something to offer in terms of expertise. And I'd have to be convinced that they knew a good deal more than I did about the life of my community."

Given the staggering growth of community foundations over the past two decades, it stands to reason that their capabilities would vary wildly. "If you've seen one community foundation, you've seen one community foundation," quipped Terence Mulligan, CEO of the Napa Valley Community Foundation. "If you're interested in forming an alliance, you should look for staff that understands what you care about and what's important in the community. Those are the two biggies. It's our job to understand what ignites the passions of the donor."

How do you tell whether the community foundation in your area might be the right partner for you?

- **Education** Community foundations should help donors grow into their roles. Does your community foundation offer a formal introduction to philanthropic practice? Does the staff regularly use presentations or publications to highlight issues, such as education, arts, or the environment? Are donors convened to swap stories, discuss their goals, and refine their skills? Does anybody show up at these events?

- **Zeal** The board and staff should be striving to do more than grow the endowment and service donor-advised funds. They should want to change the world. A colleague working within Germany's fledgling community foundation sector remarked that his associates routinely spoke of philanthropy as a "movement" to strengthen civil society. That's not a word most American funders would use. We should. But we must earn the right to do so.

- **Results** How do the board and staff make decisions about their discretionary grantmaking? How do they define success? Ask for examples. Ask about failure, too. What has been tried in the past that but proved disappointing? Even disastrous? Funders who can't point to efforts that flopped aren't trying hard enough. Or worse, they aren't learning from their experience.

- **Background** Where have the staff previously worked? Have its leaders and program officers run nonprofits themselves? (Sadly, and infuriatingly, many foundations hire staff who have never met a payroll, penned a grant application, or, more tellingly, dedicated a portion of their life to alleviating a social ill or building a valuable institution.) What does the staff know about the issues that move you? If you sit down for an hour's conversation regarding the condition of local schools or the fate of our oceans, do you walk away with your brain pleasantly abuzz? Who sits on the board? How is

the foundation governed? Who else is a donor (and would somebody please make an introduction so that can you can talk with
them about their experience)?

- **Responsiveness** Does the staff promptly return your calls?
  (Bizarrely, and maddeningly, we have encountered community
  foundations of considerable size that fail this basic test.) Do other
  donors seem satisfied with the nuts and bolts of bookkeeping
  and IRS adherence? Are their requests for information processed
  in a timely manner? Is turnover sufficiently low that you can bank
  on an abiding relationship with key staff that will deepen with
  time?

- **Staying power** Does the board have sufficient focus and determination to craft an informed strategy for improving their community,
  and then stick with it for five to ten years? Some community foundations flit from one set of goals and objectives to another in the
  same way a broker might churn your stock portfolio. Such actions
  are full of sound and fury signifying nothing but a justification for
  personnel costs. Beware of institutions that leap from one "strategic
  plan" to another. It's a sign that words count for more than deeds—
  and that somebody has confused planning with doing.

- **Community connections** Does the board and staff cultivate
  relationships with the people who do the real work of philanthropy—the nonprofit sector's most dedicated and effective professionals? How often do program officers conduct site visits?
  Are donors encouraged to undertake their own visits? Do they
  receive guidance? Does the foundation ask donors to contribute
  to a discretionary fund to handle emergencies, provide ongoing
  support to key institutions, and address long-term community needs? What do nonprofit leaders think about the attitude,
  aspirations, and performance of the community foundation?

Publicly, all funders are princes. Privately, you'll often hear a franker, darker story.

- ***Uber*-ambition** Large foundations frequently suffer from...how shall I say it? A deficit of modesty. They've got a lot of money and they come to believe that they know more than those entities and individuals who do not. This arrogance (*yes*, that's the word) can lead to ill-starred initiatives in which a foundation pounces upon a particular strategy, ploughs money into its realization for two or three years, but fails to reckon with or even consult the organizations who are already working in the field. As a result, the initiative duplicates services and ultimately destabilizes the local nonprofit community. This kind of ambition produces few lasting worthwhile results.

- **An appropriate itch** A program officer speaks frankly: "I spend a lot of time telling exceptional orgs 'No.'" He's not alone. Most requests to community foundations get denied, including dazzling projects that promise to shake up the status quo for the betterment of all. You might say, *Well, of course—there's simply not enough money swilling around in their coffers.* Not quite. In truth, vast sums are presently sitting in community foundation donor-advised funds. Just sitting. Because there's no legal requirement compelling you or the foundation to move the money out of your fund and into community use. As a donor, you bear the final burden of responsibility to get your money circulating. A good foundation partner itches to help you fulfill this responsibility. You'll get nudges, suggestions, encouragement—and lots of good ideas about great projects. A righteous ally will look beyond the management fees and compound interest that too frequently gum up the philanthropic works—and do everything possible to persuade you to turn your money into action. Not in six months or next year or sometime in the foggy future. Now.

Letting Go to Get Things Done

Let's face it. Even if you're keenly aware of your overall philanthropic aims, you still may not possess sufficient time (or interest) to decide precisely which organizations would be ideal grant recipients. In these circumstances, the only tool more useful than a savvy advisor would be a national network of savvy advisors.

Hey, presto: these networks abound!

The Funding Exchange links together sixteen public foundations around the country with its national office in New York. Together they grant nearly $15 million annually to unabashedly progressive grassroots organizations working for social change. With its affiliates widely dispersed across more than a dozen states, the Funding Exchange serves as the eyes and ears for projects and organizations that might otherwise remain hidden from most donors. Operating since 1979, the Funding Exchange is the most venerable of national networks, and a key resource for donors committed to "change, not charity" through a variety of "activist-led" grantmaking programs.

Recent decades have also seen a momentous rise in "women's funds"— affiliations of (mostly) female donors who support underfunded projects assisting women and girls at home and abroad. A report recently conducted by the Foundation Center and Women's Funding Network indicates that from 2004 to 2006, giving by women's funds grew 24 percent—surpassing the increase of overall foundation giving by nearly 10 percent. This trend is expected to continue. Women now control more than half of the nation's private wealth, stand to inherit 70 percent of the $40+ trillion intergenerational transfer anticipated over the next four decades, and, most decisively, give away their money at roughly twice the rate of men (3.5 percent versus 1.8 percent).

"Women philanthropists," noted a recent article in *Forbes*, "have long pointed to the empowerment of women and girls as a successful strategy for achieving sustained economic growth and productivity in communities around the world. Not surprisingly, it is women donors who originally took the lead in investing in women-led solutions to many of the world's greatest challenges—from climate change to food security—based on the belief that women themselves know best how to determine their needs and propose solutions for lasting change."

Donors today can join a bevy of national and international collaborators, including the Women Donors Network, the Women's Funding Network, the Global Fund for Women, and area-specific organizations such as the Central American Women's Fund, the Canadian Women's Foundation, and many others. Women's funding groups are also on the rise at state and regional levels, complementing the ranks of more established funders such as the Women's Funding Alliance in Washington state, the Iowa Women's Foundation, the Arizona Foundation for Women, and the Appalachian Women's Fund.

Beyond identifying strategic destinations for philanthropic dollars, the women involved with these funds consistently emphasize their commitment to building a new generation of informed givers. Writing on the Tactical Philanthropy Advisors website, Sara Hall of New Philanthropy Advisors recently pointed to several distinctive characteristics of women donors. "Women are willing to start at the beginning," she wrote, "allowing their energy for the mission to propel them through the earliest learning stages. They become deeply engaged in the process of learning, are willing to be perceived as novices, and tend to be open not only to ideas, but to getting things done in unconventional ways." Perhaps most important: "Women are not only willing to mentor and share, they seek opportunities to do so. They engage the community of other philanthropists, grantees, and partners, and share their stories to inspire and guide others."

My own experience among the old guard of the traditionally male-dominated foundation world leads me to agree that the new wave of women's funds marks a striking and important development in philanthropy. I'm thinking now about a conference I attended a few years ago, where I was one of a handful of men participating in a break-out session on women's funding. Early into the session, we were asked to divide into small groups, discuss our funding goals, and then report back to the full gathering. It's a common enough method, and I can't begin to count the times I've been worked through similar paces. But the women participating in this conference took the prospect of forging new connections with the utmost seriousness—and, tellingly, with an attendant sense of discovery and joy. Conversations proved deeply personal, emotional, trusting, buoyant, risky. Sure, we hear these words trotted out now and then in discussions of what grantmaking *should* be. But this was the genuine article: personal connections in the service of practical collaboration. To my eyes, it seemed a messier, richer, more complex and authentic way of thinking about philanthropy and then turning those thoughts into action.

If we desire any more evidence about the importance of networks, we need only consider the now-legendary Women Moving Millions campaign. Launched during the brunt of our recent Great Recession, when individual giving suffered the steepest one-year decline on record, the campaign managed to exceed its goal of raising $150 million for women and girls by more than $30 million, with donors each giving $1 million or more. Rather than reinventing the wheel—or forming new foundations—this battery of significant givers linked arms, relied upon one another, and put to excellent use a prodigious amount of money. Their achievement shows us all what can be done when teamwork becomes a reality.

Rating Wealth Advisors

Since the economic boom of the 1990s, philanthropy has drawn increasing attention from banks, investment houses, insurance companies, and other for-profit ventures that have shrewdly recognized a growing market among aspiring donors. Big names in finance have entered the field, with Morgan Stanley, Fidelity, and Wells Fargo among the brand names setting themselves up as philanthropic advisors. According to Fidelity, its Gift Fund has worked with more than 56,000 donors since 1991, recommending more than $10 billion in grants to over 136,000 nonprofit organizations. Without a doubt, the market savvy, professionalism, and ready access to wealthy individuals will help the financial sector to expand its philanthropic interests in coming years.

But while financial institutions are well disposed to handle the legal, fiscal, and reporting requirements, their qualifications for advising donors *where* to give remains dubious. Guidance within most financial services institutions unsurprisingly focuses on the financial aspects of charitable tools and tax benefits. The donor who wants his giving to reach beyond the usual suspects—the alma mater, house of worship, and disease of choice—will have to seek assistance elsewhere.

Into this breach has stepped an array of professional wealth advisors who directly serve individual donors without the organizational trappings of an investment firm or community foundation. Like most professions that spring suddenly from unregulated opportunity, there's no credentialing process or even firm agreement about responsibilities and required skills. Naturally, the advisors' backgrounds, abilities, knowledge, motivations, and performance range from top-notch to dreary. How can you tell the difference between an advisor with the right credentials and everybody else?

Here are a few questions you might ask:

- **Philanthropic pedigree** Where did the advisor spend his working day before hanging out a shingle for private practice? The foundation world? (Great. But what does he know about nonprofits?) The nonprofit field? (Interesting. But does he understand the tools and legal requirements of philanthropy?) The business world? (When and how did he accrue sufficient understanding of both the independent and philanthropic sectors?) Provenance counts. You'll pay a pretty penny for professional advice. Makes sure it's coming from someone who can rightly lay claim to the profession.

- **Social benefit** How has the advisor's work made a difference, and not just as an advisor (we'll get to that)? Rather, how have her professional and volunteer activities over the years helped create a more just, abundant, and beautiful world? Dependable advisors speak from experience. They've invested their own sweat equity in the kinds of projects they can be proud of, and they've learned from their experiences, both good and bad. Be dubious about any advisor who hasn't pitched in personally.

- **Feeling tone** What does your gut say? How would you characterize your first meeting? (Are you inclined towards a second?) Do you feel comfortable speaking candidly with the advisor about your money, family, aspirations, and fears? Do you like him? Can you imagine inviting him to your home—perhaps numerous times over many years? A wealth advisor is essentially a family practitioner, like a family doctor or lawyer. Trust is the bedrock.

- **Execution** What are the steps you'll be taking in working together? How much time will it require? What will the costs be?

- **History** Explore the basics: What's the best grant the advisor has recommended? The worst? How have both experiences influenced her work as an advisor?

- **Territory** Bid the advisor to wax cogently about the fields that interest you most. About the communities you want to support. About the problems and opportunities that he foresees and you can't. How does the advisor keep up to date with developments in the nonprofit sector? Within the geographical region you want to support? Who does he know that you don't, and who does he plan to meet? Highly analytical people are often drawn to philanthropy. Does your prospective advisor also possess the energy, interest, and moxie to deliver on the requisite shoe-leather research? A thorough investigation of funding opportunities can't be conducted exclusively by telephone—or worse, online. To learn about the world, you have to step into it with eyes and heart wide open.

- **Results** How does the advisor define success? How will your giving improve? What else will have changed because of your relationship with the advisor? What immediate results can you expect to see? How much time will it take to recognize the long-term effects?

- **References** Ask for the names of three people the advisor has worked with in the past. Give them a call. Better yet, sit down with each person for an hour's conversation about their own giving and how the use of an advisor has affected their actions. Strive to maintain that delicate balance between openness and skepticism, knowing that your experience will almost certainly differ from those of the advisor's most and least satisfied clients.

Your Side of the Partnership

Until now, we've been talking about the requisite qualities of professional advisors and funding partners. But they're only one side of the equation— the one that donors have the least power to change. The more tantalizing prospects for learning and engagement reside on the donor's end.

"Most donors don't see their giving in a strategic way," acknowledged an experienced advisor to family foundations and individual donors interested in social justice and environmental issues. "They want to give, get the good feeling, and benefit from the tax write-off. But it's a bit of a chore. What's required of them isn't immediately apparent."

What does it take to be an informed and conscious donor working in partnership with a seasoned intermediary?

- **Open ears** The best funders are good listeners. They know the difference between a conversation and a monologue, and prefer the former.

- **Constant curiosity** They're perpetual learners, eager to study the issues and master the context. They reject pat answers and maintain an open mind.

- **Patience** Change takes time, and good funders stick it out. Most problems that seem intractable are simply on a course of slow-motion change. Remember, funders backed anti-Apartheid activists for twenty years before the issue gained traction.

- **Realism** Effectiveness is sometimes a matter of luck, being at the right place at the right time. Not everything you attempt will reap the desired results.

Finally, conscious donors recognize that money alone won't build the kind of world they desire. So they pitch in personally—as advocates, volunteers, board members. They experiment. If one method of reaching people in need doesn't work, they'll try another. They see themselves as part of something much larger than their own family, neighborhood, state, or nation. They're part of our vast, disorderly, tragic, beautiful, irrepressible world of possibilities and disappointments—with responsibilities to people and places they'll never personally encounter. In their special role as philanthropists, they're willing to change whatever isn't working in order to put their money where it's needed most.

During my years in philanthropy, I've come to believe that the most effective donors start with a strong sense of purpose. Then they allow their earliest conception of giving to evolve. They take pains to avoid isolation, involving their friends and loved ones in research and decision making. They cultivate new colleagues whose knowledge, counsel, and judgment they trust. They recognize that they'll never have enough hours in the day or years in their lives to get everything done that needs doing. So they reach out. Tapping into networks, searching for new intermediaries, hiring advisors, seeking aid wherever it dwells. It's what keeps them attentive, stimulated, happy, committed—and useful.

3

The Value of the Undramatic Gesture

Principle #3 *Dare to be dull.*

Donors are frequently drawn to the dramatic gesture. They underwrite a gorgeous new performing arts center bearing their name. They declare their personal animus towards an intransigent social ill or crippling disease and then pour resources into its eradication. They fund a groundbreaking program trumpeted by a high-profile organization—and rightly feel invigorated by the tangible effort and quantifiable results.

Which is all to the good. We need bolder, more courageous giving. And we'll argue for just such an approach in the next chapter.

But for now, I want to sing the praises of unspectacular philanthropy. The kind of giving that doesn't establish reputations or inspire banner headlines. An approach to funding that some people might even consider—well…boring.

Except it isn't.

What I'm talking about is grantmaking that has less to do with the poetry of grand ambitions than the prosaic need to brace and fortify the nonprofit sector.

It's not really dull at all. It's simply a subtler style.

Uncelebrated.

Often neglected.

And essential.

Your Best Investment in the Nonprofit Sector: General Operating Support

Over the years, I've come to understand that what most productive, well-run nonprofits need isn't another round of program funding. Or a seed grant to explore new directions. Or any other splashy, attention-getting gift that fires the imagination of the local funding community and spawns a crew of imitators. What most nonprofits crave, require, and rarely receive is gobs of discretionary money to cover general operating expenses. Either for the organization as a whole or, in the case of large, multifaceted groups, no-strings support to pursue a particular issue.

General operating support keeps the telephones ringing and the electricity flowing. It pays for printer cartridges and the Internet server along with rent, insurance, and biannual visits from the elevator service technician. It helps cover salaries, benefits, postage, travel, and per diem. In a perfect world, it might even add a smidgen to the organizational reserve. Nonprofits must look to general operating support for all the expenditures on administration, plant maintenance, technology, and fundraising that most foundations, government agencies, and individual donors don't want to pay for. All those unromantic goods and services that allow the agency to pursue its mission.

In times of want and uncertainty, discretionary funding is particularly welcome. Fortunately, some donors intuitively grasp this need.

"When the economic meltdown occurred," one seasoned donor told us, "we decided that we'd keep funding the organizations we had supported in the past, but we'd make it all discretionary money. They were like family. This was no time to cut them off or complicate their work with restrictions."

There's little disagreement about the importance of general operating support. In a series of national focus groups convened by Grantmakers for Effective Organizations, funders and nonprofit representatives identified increasing such support as "one of the most effective changes grantmakers could make to improve nonprofit results." Other research confirms this finding. In 2006, a survey of nearly two thousand nonprofit executives (conducted by CompassPoint Nonprofit Services and the Eugene and Agnes E. Meyer Foundation) rated general operating support as the most effective tool that funders could use in aiding the nonprofit sector's work. Just ask any executive. Without the working capital to sustain daily operations, disaster looms.

"You need lights, you need water, you need stamps," declared a donor who has over the years steadily increased her unrestricted giving. "We couldn't run our businesses without being able to pay for these basics. Why should we expect nonprofits to do so?"

In some ways, individual donors who have struggled to make ends meet in the business world may be better prepared to grasp the need for unrestricted funds than their peers at better-heeled foundations and government agencies. When I was a foundation executive, I certainly worried about the health of our endowment and our ability to continue making significant grants in multiple areas. But there was never a moment when I feared that we wouldn't be able to cover our payroll or that I'd have to start hauling home garbage in the trunk of my car because we could no longer afford to pay for municipal trash collection. Nonprofits regularly face these kinds of pressures. Most people outside the sector have little sense of the constant juggling of resources that so many valued community institutions must perform behind closed doors.

Individual donors who provide general operating support can help alleviate some of this pressure. Unrestricted funds liberate executives from the endless grind of fundraising so they can focus instead on pro-grams and attend to the overarching need of building a durable, resilient organization. They allow nonprofits to take calculated risks and recover from setbacks. They provide the inestimable gift of time—not weeks or months, but years—so the organization can develop breadth and depth of leadership. General operating support treats nonprofit professionals like grown-ups, instead of doling out restricted monies with the infantilizing overcautiousness of an allowance. It vests responsibility for spending deci-sions where it should reside: with the executive and an engaged board.

It says: I believe in your mission, your plan, your commitment, and your judgment—so good luck!

Yet many funders blanch at the notion of paying for "overhead" or "administration." They want their money to support "programs"—as though programs could somehow leap fully formed from disembodied goodwill and aspiration. "Restricted giving misses a fundamental point," argues Jim Collins in his monograph, *Good to Great and the Social Sectors.* "To make the greatest impact on society requires first and foremost a great organization, not a single great program."

If we don't underwrite general operating expenses, we ensure a weak and wobbly nonprofit sector. It will burn out the best people, perform erratically, and waste much of the money so consciously dedicated to programming. Every gift that arrives wrapped up in strings further com-promises the long-term promise of effectiveness.

By concentrating too much on program grants, donors also entice non-profit leaders down the treacherous path of deception and self-delusion. All too aware of funders' preferences, executives may leap at money earmarked for activities they have no business pursuing. Or they may contort their existing programs to catch a funder's eye. In the end, they will only com-pound their own financial difficulties by underestimating overhead costs. Eventually, the trap snaps shut. The organization finds itself locked into a host of programming commitments with no way to turn on the lights.

We all know that today's nonprofit sector is hugely and systematically undercapitalized. But it can get even worse. In recent years, misguided marketers and sector watchdogs have seduced donors with brassy declarations about subliminal overhead. Some nonprofits boast about budgeting a ruinous 5 percent for administration with the rest allegedly dedicated to programs. For most organizations, spending 95 percent of your money on programs is dangerous—if even possible. Sure, now and then some sinewy volunteer group will manage to pull it off. Still, the more likely scenario falls along the lines of a theater company devoting the bulk of its resources to commissioning a play, but failing to pay its actors, hire stage hands, advertise the performances—or install an alarm system for when the inevitable fire breaks out. It's a deadly strategy that strains credulity and establishes an irresponsible standard for the sector.

A Strategy of Steadiness

Nonprofit executives routinely manage a dozen restricted grants and government contracts. In effect, they're saddled with the equivalent of a dozen bosses, each specifying the percentage of the grant that may be used for lights, water, rent, salaries, and the like. It's maddening.

Your gift of discretionary funding awarded over multiple years can help make for a saner situation. But first, you need to carefully examine your own reasons for giving.

Some donors crave acknowledgment in terms of visible concrete outcomes. A program, a playing field, a new hospital wing bearing their name. You might be primarily interested in public recognition—even that's no sin. (Keep in mind the 2,500 Carnegie libraries still freckling the map.) If so, you may find ongoing support for a stalwart organization a hard notion to swallow. Not everybody can feature himself as the guy who paid for this year's liability insurance or the gal who's keeping the bookkeeper glued to his desk by stickily underwriting his health coverage. Perhaps it's best for discretionary donors to gloss over the specifics of their donation's ultimate end. Try to regard your contribution as a discrete piece of the organizational slab that enables the spires and bell towers to soar. In setting your own cornerstone of unrestricted support, you're assuming the critical work shunned by most other funders.

I only wish the foundation world would devote a much larger share of its resources to general operating support. While it's critical to support excellent programs over the years, I'm also proud of every unrestricted dollar the Packard Foundation has put into the hands of dynamic organizations who understand their needs and priorities much better than our staff and board members would ever be able to do. But I also recognize that the foundation world isn't going to change overnight. Despite greater openness to long-term grantmaking designed to assist key institutions in establishing themselves over many years, large foundations continue to be stirred and occasionally seduced by the allure of innovation and experimentation—the ceaseless pursuit of the new.

That means individual donors can and should now step into the breach to play a significant role in securing the nonprofit sector.

Of course, the most critical task is choosing the right organization to back for the long haul. In the foundation and business world, this process is referred to as due diligence. It's usually a time-consuming labor involving a multiplicity of steps. Foundations attempting to identify their best investments usually conduct a rigorous data analysis, peer into the overall health of the organization, talk with other funders, and then rely on their well-informed instincts.

Your own process—as with many aspects of giving—should not emulate the big foundations. As an individual donor or small family foundation, you have neither the time, personnel, interest, or need to conduct an extensive inquiry into every gift. What should concern you is the presence of the basic building blocks of a good nonprofit.

Look for:

- **A capable executive** A successful organization depends on a director with sufficient skills and dedication to handle a dozen tasks simultaneously. Keep your eyes open for brains, grace, balance, determination, and verve. Without keen vision and stable management, nothing can be accomplished.

- **Depth of leadership** If an organization is going to survive beyond the reign of its charismatic founder, it must cultivate leadership at multiple levels. In the end, leadership has less to do with any one person than with an organizational attitude that rewards initiative and responsibility, while providing opportunities for professional growth.

- **An engaged board** The trustees should set the organization's mission, oversee finances, throw their back into the unending task of fundraising, and otherwise assist the leadership in marching towards their goals. The board should neither fall prey to micromanagement nor regard its duties as pro forma. Membership on a healthy nonprofit board can often be a demanding part-time job.

- **The active pursuit of a realistic development plan** Your gift, no matter how significant, is only a single slice of the funding pie. For a nonprofit to survive over the long run, it needs the participation of the executive, the engagement of the board, and probably at least one staffer dedicated to raising money. Goals have to be set, charted, pursued—and then realigned to meet the shifting sands of reality.

- **Reliable financial management** You shouldn't need an accounting background to interpret the fiscal state of your favored organization. Scan the annual budget and the previous year's financial statement, ask about cost controls, find out how data analysis informs policy at both the executive and board levels. But make it a conversation, not an interrogation. Comprehension will emerge from an honest and ongoing exchange.

- **A compelling reason for existence** Do programs lead to the desired outcomes? Can the leaders articulate their mission beyond half-baked homilies and clunky code words? Who would notice if the organization suddenly ceased to be? Are the end results really worth all the blood, sweat, and tears?

- **The ability to grow** Does the organization remain in touch with its constituency so that it understands the changing context of its work? Does it have the capacity to adapt to new circumstances and steadily improve its performance?

To explore these qualities, you'll need to rely on your analytical abilities, observational prowess, and sheer gut instinct—just like you do in every human encounter. Unfortunately, many nonprofits have been trained by the foundation world to respond to inquiries with a document dump. Ask for info and you're liable to be handed the sundry gilt-edged array of annual reports, board rosters, committee minutes, 990s, organizational charts, multiple copies of multiple proposals, and heaps of plans. You're not going to read them. You don't need to read them.

Genuine due diligence doesn't result from an accumulation of paper. It isn't an artifact, much less an event. Rather, it evolves over time as a process, an outcome of your ongoing relationship with an organization. It derives from openness and persistence. The more time you're willing to invest in learning about any nonprofit, the better your investments in the sector will be. Your powers of perception will grow increasingly acute. You'll be able to decode the cumbersome jargon and prick up your ears to the sound of baloney. You'll be building a basis for good judgment by accruing the bedrock of experience from which reliable instincts eventually spring.

In Praise of Gradual Progress

If all this sounds like a lot of work with little fanfare, then I believe you have grasped my point. Earthquakes and hurricanes take place overnight. Progress trundles along at a tortoise's pace. As funders, our actions must reflect this truth in timing.

Consider the common nonprofit statement of purpose. An idealistic, capable young organization may proclaim its animating vision to be "a world without poverty." But no matter how hard and long they work, that goal will probably remain elusive. Is it worth struggling for? Of course. Countless individuals and organizations have over the centuries dedicated their existence to alleviating poverty, and most historians employing multiple points of comparison would agree that they've made progress. Millions of ordinary people now live in a state of everyday splendor that would have beggared the imagination of the wealthiest nineteenth-century plutocrat and made Croesus blush. Do we still face hunger, want, and yawning gaps between the wealthy and the poor? We do. But step by step, throughout the elaborate, sometimes agonizing process of building civilization, the material conditions of ordinary people have substantially improved. Certainly, that's true for the industrialized (and now postindustrialized) societies—and we can all see India, China, and Brazil now reshaping their corners of the globe.

That's how incrementalism works. Relentless hard work produces modest improvements that the next generation takes as its imperfect starting point and then builds upon. And every generation needs the support of generous, dedicated individuals with time, talent, and money.

After many years of watching countless plans for instant transformation run out of fuel, I now embrace incrementalism as one of philanthropy's orienting truths. Little changes for the good quickly. Unless we're willing to support the steady work of our nonprofit partners, then not much will change period.

That means funding original ideas, daring initiatives, visionary leaders. But it also means maintaining a baseline of dependable support for key institutions, both locally and beyond. I'd much rather make a grant to a reliable stalwart in my community than fall into the trap of trendy giving dictated by whatever new theory, spokesperson, or untested tool has arrived on the scene. I think we have to stand alongside establishment nonprofits—as long as they're still being productive. How to make them increasingly productive is the next challenge in no-frills funding.

The Steady Drip-Drip-Drip of Time and Money

For many years, the president of a small Catholic college had been courting a major donor. In the past, the donor had given modestly, if erratically. The president hoped to lure him into the inner circle of major supporters with a large, single gift focused on some array of overarching needs and splendid opportunities that would prove irresistible. But the time never seemed ripe to pop the question. The president waited several years for the perfect moment to announce itself. After all, the donor appeared healthy, vital, and young at heart, if not green in years.

Eventually, the president plucked up her courage and resolved to make her pitch the very next week. A national conference took her out of town for several days. When she returned, she attended Sunday mass and heard the bad news from the pulpit: "Let us pray," intoned the priest solemnly, "for the repose of the soul...." The donor had died peacefully in his sleep the night before.

"It's consistency that matters," said the director of a large nonprofit when she heard this story. "I'd rather have smaller grants over the years than one large donation where I have to

jump through a lot of hoops. I want to be able to budget, anticipate income, know where my gaps will be. If I can count on a
small, solid amount every year, then I don't have to go crazy
seeking these big gifts that too often never materialize."

Consistency is a virtue. It holds back the floodwaters.
It also hints pleasingly at the possibility of increase.

"If somebody gives $1,000 over five years," said a nonprofit
fundraiser, "then I can see they've thought about us, they're
committed, and they have some means. On the sixth year, if I
can make my case, they might consider giving $5,000. When
we get to know each other better, the amount could grow to
$10,000. But the real point, whether there's growth or not, is
that these gifts are accumulating. We keep track of our donors'
contributions over a lifetime, and we show them what it adds
up to. They're usually astonished. They'll say, 'I don't think of
myself as somebody who gives away ten, or fifteen, or twenty
thousand dollars.' But over time, they have. They see how much
of a contribution they've really made, and we acknowledge how
important that kind of steadiness has been to us. It points to our
partnership. We're tied together by dollars multiplied by time,
and the result is gratifying for us all."

Forging a Stronger, Smarter Sector

I entered the world of philanthropy through an oddly placed door. After
earning my MBA at Stanford, I worked for a number of years in international banking. I acquired the tools needed for rigorous financial analysis.
I absorbed the demanding work ethic of the field. Most important, I benefitted daily by meeting people from around the world whose experiences

and points of view differed from my own by almost unimaginable measures. This immersion in complexity helped me make the transition to the foundation world, where there seldom exists a single correct answer to any problem.

Looking back, I don't think I could have planned a better route for my career in philanthropy. But I'm also aware of what I didn't understand as I made the transition. Like most people steeped in the ethos, tools, perspective, and methods of the business world, I didn't begin to grasp the challenges faced by the people running nonprofit organizations.

I'm not alone.

How many times have you heard a well-meaning board member or volunteer utter the familiar complaint *If this nonprofit were run more like a business, all its problems would be solved?*

Give that same person six months of close-quarters acquaintance inside the guts of a nonprofit and they'll almost always come back whistling a different tune.

It's more complicated than I thought…

Nonprofit leaders face problems we never have to consider…

How do they manage to go on?

Of course, nonprofits aren't businesses. They operate with an entirely different bottom line. The central question is not How much money have we made for our investors? Rather, it's How much good have we accomplished?

And at what cost?

And how long will it last?

I think the value we're really discussing is professionalism.

When nonprofits conduct their operations with knowledge, skill, and grasp of the larger picture—as trained professionals—then many of the seemingly intransigent problems inside the organization eventually do get solved.

But how do hectic, cash-poor nonprofits acquire the training they need?

Even today, many nonprofit leaders accidentally stumble into their positions of authority, with the sector's demands thrust upon them by a sudden shift in staffing or the eruption of a fiscal crisis. They learn by doing—on-the-job training conducted in a pressure cooker of rising need and unreliable resources. It's not the best way to absorb critical skills, but for too many people over too many years, it's been the usual way.

Fortunately, numerous sources for professional development have become more accessible in recent years. One area of dramatic growth: academia. Today almost three hundred colleges and universities offer courses in nonprofit management—a rarity on campuses even twenty years ago. Of these, 168 run graduate programs with a concentration in nonprofit management.

Any one of them might be a logical place to park a substantial sum dedicated to training a new generation of nonprofit leaders.

Or you can act locally by supporting your favorite nonprofit so that it can hire one of the many excellent technical assistance organizations that have cropped up throughout the nation. The best of these groups hire seasoned consultants with real-world experience to teach nonprofits how to identify their goals, plan their programs, create a working budget and analyze financial data, harness technology, master fundraising, build a better board, and supervise staff. With workshops, study circles, publications, tools, and direct consultation, these experts in their fields pass on the knowledge required to handle the full range of tasks that staff must otherwise pick up on the run.

Personally, I'm sold on this kind of support. It's intimate, tailored to personal and organizational needs, and relatively inexpensive to deliver. At Packard, we funded the organizational effectiveness of our grantees for many years, providing them with funds to hire technical assistance consultants of their choice in addition to their program grants, so they didn't feel like they had to choose between, say, protecting wetlands and training their new bookkeeper. Dollar for dollar, I still think it's some of the best grantmaking we undertook, since it served as an insurance policy protecting our overall investments. We didn't have to worry about grafting the strong arm of an exemplary program onto the weak body of an organization—a dismayingly common occurrence that usually ends badly. We knew that by improving the skills of key staff and gradually raising the bar on professional expectations, we were contributing agency by agency to a stronger, smarter, and more reflective nonprofit sector.

It stands to reason that an organization with strong leadership and oversight is more likely to achieve its program goals. But I'm not referring exclusively to improvements in management. An organization can operate quite efficiently—raising money, balancing the books, keeping staff and board happily employed—without being effective. Effectiveness in the nonprofit realm is about creating positive, sustainable change. Making waves. Even launching tsunamis. In order to secure significant changes, nonprofits must marry sound management and governance to vision and imagination. They must be able to articulate their mission, set goals, and then align their strategies. Organizational effectiveness takes time, usually years. And it requires somebody other than the nonprofits to pick up the tab.

Nonprofits and organized philanthropy generally give lip service to the importance of improving skills and introducing new tools and concepts. But they seldom provide sufficient resources. That's a shame. Because every organization, no matter how well it's run, will eventually face challenges. Indeed, disruptions and even temporary crises are the logical result of an organization growing, taking risks, and coping with events in the world beyond its control. Healthy organizations address these challenges head-on. It's a sign of their strength.

These days, the foundation world has warmed to the idea of supporting the professional development of the nonprofit sector. Individual donors have proven somewhat slower to join the venture.

"Most want to focus on programs," said one donor, "not on infrastructure. In the business world, everyone understands that something like information technology or leadership recruitment is a regular, recurring expense. They invest. They realize that there's no choice if they're going to survive. We should learn from their example."

How can donors buoy the skills of their local nonprofit community?

One fruitful tactic is to support the outstanding technical assistance organizations working at subsidized, below-market rates. Invariably, these groups are nonprofits themselves, as dependent on fundraising as the agencies they assist and just as hungry for reliable, no-strings cash. In the San Francisco Bay Area, nonprofits almost inevitably turn for help to CompassPoint Nonprofit Services, which has set the standard for consulting, workshops, and authoritative publications. In Boston, Third Sector New England performs at a similar high level, serving nonprofits and unincorporated groups determined to build capacity for the long haul. You can seek out the technical assistance leaders in your own region with a few quick phone calls to your local community foundation, United Way, or university nonprofit program. Or consult a few of the nonprofits you most respect, and ask who they turn to for solid training and advice. You'll rapidly find a consensus emerging about who's doing the best work in your community.

A more imaginative wrinkle on bolstering the long-term strength of the local voluntary network is suggested by Jan Masaoka, publisher of the engaging online nonprofit newsletter *Blue Avocado*, and one of shrewdest observers of the sector.

"I'd consider shining a light on the everyday heroes working in nonprofits with an awards program," she said. "Set up a structure to identify five outstanding financial officers, or development directors, or informational technology specialists. Or folks working on the front lines—social workers, clinical nurses, or the person on the other end of an emergency hotline. Staff who don't usually get a lot of public notice. The award needs to be large enough to leverage attention—say, a thousand dollars—and the ceremonies should be conducted at city hall. Get the mayor involved; make it an event. You'll honor key individuals, create interest in their work, and highlight the issues and skills that are their specialty. You'll underscore the sense that this work is important and valued. You might even inspire people to enter the field."

Variations on this theme abound. You could host a reception at city hall to recognize the city's emerging nonprofit executives—young people at the beginning of their careers who haven't received much public notice, despite their contributions. The event might furnish some interesting networking possibilities among professionals who famously fail to make one another's acquaintance in even the most robust nonprofit hubs. As important, you'll be making visible the unacknowledged leadership of your community. Be sure to hire a photographer for a group portrait, and make certain that the image is widely disseminated—in the press, on the web, and in the offices of everybody in attendance.

"It could be like Art Kane's famous photo of New York's jazz musicians in 1958," mused Jan. " 'A Great Day in Harlem' with Thelonious Monk, Sonny Rollins, and fifty other masters from that era. Only you'd be featuring one great day in the nonprofit sector of your city."

Public recognition can go a long way towards making certain that outstanding staff get sufficient encouragement and support to remain in their jobs. Studies show that the executive's tenure is a principal factor in an organization achieving a high level of effectiveness. "There are times," summarized one funder, "when the most important contribution you can make is ensuring that a strong executive will remain on the job for the next five years. With that person in place, you know the group will make progress."

Continuity at the top levels of management is essential if we're to weather the storms that may soon shake the sector. Most perilously, we now find ourselves on the cusp of a leadership crisis. The precipitating factors? The retirement of baby boomers, the further retrenchment of state and federal funding, and an increasing demand for services. In its study "The Nonprofit Sector's Leadership Deficit," the Bridgespan Group found that the sector will need 640,000 new leaders within the coming decade—more than twice the existing number of positions. Where will these leaders come from if nonprofits are known primarily for their poor pay, meager benefits, and soul-numbing expectations for perpetual fundraising? Who wants to devote his or her career to a prolonged, uncelebrated exercise in privation? Given all the hardships and difficulties, will the nonprofit sector be viewed as a rewarding and interesting enough place for talented people to spend their lives?

The Most Interesting Work in the World

Which brings us back to that four-letter word: dull.

Dull is precisely what your steady support for the nonprofit sector should not be. Undramatic and unspectacular, yes. Unnoticed by others, perhaps. But if you find yourself bored by your own efforts to sustain an outstanding nonprofit over the years, then something's wrong. Perhaps it's your choice of organization. Maybe it's your own unconscious desire for formal recognition or high-level involvement in shaping goals and policies. Perhaps you've been following funding trends too closely, or listening to the advice of your big sister or little brother rather than your own heart. In any case, there's a problem. Because philanthropy should not be dreary and dull. It can't be, if it's to be sustained over many years—which should be our goal. Philanthropy is a way of renewing the world. It's how we improve on what we find during our life's short span, leaving something for the next generation to make even better. It should be stimulating. A pleasure. An adventure.

My own experience tells me that it can even be thrilling.

I'm thinking now about our efforts at the Packard Foundation to help our grantees increase their own effectiveness. When we first started out, I remember one nonprofit executive telling me that if his agency were a college student and the subject they were trying to master were management and governance, they would probably wind up with a C+. Then he looked me in the eye and boldly announced: "I'm aiming for an A minus."

Now perhaps that sounds silly to some ears. Can you really characterize a complex organization's aims and operations with that imperfect bit of archaic symbolism, the letter grade? But what I heard in that executive's voice was the sound of realism and a passion to improve. Like most nonprofit leaders, he was hungry for new skills and understanding.

We provided some money for the group to hire a consultant who worked with staff and board on planning, fiscal analysis, and fundraising. And soon, though not immediately, things began to improve. The executive could see it, the board could see it. I saw it, too. Within five years, the agency had revamped its management and governance, while sufficiently advancing its mission, so that it seemed as if we were supporting an entirely different organization. Bolder, more confident, skilled in anticipating dangers and responding to opportunities. An organization primed for survival.

Occasionally, I find myself thinking about this work, and I'll start grinning.

Slowly, sparingly, but certainly, we helped build a stronger voluntary sector by enabling individual nonprofits to improve their overall performance. We backed the organizations we believed most critical to our shared mission of protecting the environment, safeguarding women's health and reproductive rights, and improving education. In turn, the organizations achieved victories, extended their reach, strengthened themselves for the long haul. It wasn't the kind of work that people usually envision when they think about philanthropy. But I knew just how important this kind of effort could be.

And that was thrilling, too.

4

Taking Chances

Principle #4 *Embrace courage, ambiguity, discomfort, and risk.*

"Last year," remembered Ellie Friedman, "my favorite gift was in support of a film. And I don't fund films. I made that very clear to the filmmaker." Ellie laughed, and then released a comical sigh. "But I saw the early rushes and so the director got into the sanctum—she got a meeting. You know you're in trouble, so to speak, when you let someone through that door.

"I explained that I didn't have the kind of money filmmakers need, but she insisted they were only looking for support in $5,000 increments. To be truthful, the film scared me. It concerned the Israel–Palestinian conflict—from the Palestinian side. But I figured since I was scared, maybe I needed to consider the project.

"If the red flag of fear comes up," emphasized Ellie, drawing upon years of experience as a donor who values courage in grantmaking, "that's a signal you're about to learn something.

"Go there."

Along with a small cadre of funders, Ellie helped underwrite director Julia Bacha's *Budrus*, a documentary tracing the struggles of a Palestinian father and daughter who launch a nonviolent movement to save their village from destruction by Israel's Separation Barrier. Neither romanticizing the conflict nor dwelling exclusively on the suffering of victims, the film embraced an expansive view of possibilities in the Middle East.

In terms of critical reception, *Budrus* rewarded everyone's contributions. The film won festival prizes in Berlin, Jerusalem, Madrid, and San Francisco, as well as the prestigious Tribeca and Silverdocs Film Festivals. It was tapped for screenings at film gatherings in Italy, Greece, England, Australia, Turkey, Kosovo, Korea, Brazil, Norway, and India. In a keynote address immediately following the film's world premiere at the Dubai International Film Festival, Her Majesty Queen Noor Al Hussein of Jordan praised *Budrus*, emphasizing that the film "gives an enormous amount of hope....It's a story which will have an impact and can help bring change."

Of course, "change" is practically a sacred term in the parlance of grantmaking. (Who brags about their efforts to thwart it?) Yet, the inevitable handmaidens of change—controversy and opposition—are the last things most donors want to inspire. For Ellie, the perceived hazards of the grant—the very real possibilities of public failure, rancorous dissent, and clamorous denunciation—stood out as a prime selling point. She sized up the risks and plowed ahead.

"I was scared of the responsibility when I started out in philanthropy," she remembered. "What's enough to give? How do I know it's going to make a difference? Do I really want to be identified as a donor? Once word of your giving becomes public, people do come looking for support. But donors need to remember that it's not easy for those asking for money, either. We need more openness in what we're willing to entertain as funding possibilities. We have to stretch ourselves. Maybe that's the hardest part. Now I'm so proud to have helped to make this film. But I had to be willing to take a chance."

Ellie paused for a moment and then nicely summed up her years of courageous giving with an unconventional formula:

"'If you're not losing 20 percent of money you're giving away, you're not risking enough.' That's what John May, the former president of the San Francisco Foundation, used to say. I think it's an excellent principle for donors to keep in mind."

What We Mean When We Talk About Risk

Risk is a virtue. Occasional failures are inevitable. I remember Bill Hewlett making this point at Hewlett-Packard when he talked about innovation in technology. Invention calls for daring, he insisted. The meek are rarely rewarded.

At the Packard Foundation, Dave Packard similarly enjoined us to THINK BIG. In fact, it's one of the foundation's formal values adopted by the board. Part of thinking big involves calculating the risks involved, and then engaging them with open eyes and a fierce heart. It doesn't guarantee success. But to my mind, it's one of the constituent parts of progress.

"If I find ten thousand ways something won't work," declared Thomas Edison, "I haven't failed. I am not discouraged, because every wrong attempt discarded is another step forward."

Personally, I want a batting average well above one in ten thousand. But I still admire the spirit of Edison's quip. Though famously hostile to higher math and scientific method (Nikola Tesla decried Edison's "trusting himself entirely to his inventor's instinct and practical American sense"), the Wizard of Menlo Park nevertheless embodies the can-do spirit that philanthropy direly needs. In the social sphere, as with the scientific and commercial, fear usually strikes out.

But let's return for a moment to that word we've been batting about like a hot potato: *risk*. (Can't you see the steam rising from its four incendiary letters?) Though I'll argue all day that we need more courageous giving, I also want to admit right now that risk is something of a misnomer when it comes to philanthropy.

After all, what are you really risking when you make a grant whose success cannot be guaranteed?

Unlike investors introducing a new product or design, you won't take a significant financial hit. All you can lose is your gift. And even then, you haven't *lost* it. It's been put to use, even if the outcome disappoints. (And even then, you'll have whatever write-off is allowed by the IRS.)

Unlike the nonprofits working on the front lines, you haven't personally devoted countless hours to the cause that cannot be redeemed. You aren't jeopardizing your career. Your reputation probably won't even suffer. Unless you've donated a breathtaking amount, most people won't know anything about the gift's efficacy. Like it or not, the vast majority of voluntary projects flourish or fizz out in the shadows.

To my mind, there's usually only one real risk, and it's almost never discussed in relation to giving. Your biggest challenge as a donor lies in the emotional realm. You may end up feeling somebody else's pain—*really* feeling it. Courageous giving can connect you viscerally to the suffering of this world. Not in terms of abstract humanity, but with flesh-and-blood individuals. You'll be reminded on some level that despite your present ability to lend a hand, you, too, are fragile, fallible, mortal. In a word, human. And like all humans, you will age, sicken, and die.

Of course, we can shield our eyes from our own inevitable end—along with the pain and want experienced by so many individuals. But that's hardly a way to live.

Fortunately, we fallible and frightened humans also come equipped with enormous visionary potential and the capacity for hard work. Giving makes us aware of our responsibility to invest even more of ourselves in the ongoing project of diminishing pain and enlarging opportunity, beauty, justice, and joy. That's the real risk, and it's a glorious one. By embracing discomfort and uncertainty—by doing more than we imagined we might—we may well transform ourselves as well as the world.

Still, most philanthropy cannot be characterized as courageous. More often, it's convenient, predictable, unobjectionable. A no-fuss affair. So what discourages bolder giving?

• Fear of Standing Alone

When you make your annual donation to your alma mater or house of worship, you join with others in a sanctioned act of conventional charity. You run little risk of censure. Few will prove even mildly curious about the reasons you give. It's all part of the social fabric, a conventional aspect of a privileged life.

A more courageous gift is by definition less likely to be universally · esteemed. People may consider your funding decisions wasteful, foolish, even offensive or harmful. Self-doubts may arise. You may summon unwanted attention and feel yourself sticking out like a sore thumb waiting for the hammer of public opinion to come crashing down on your most sensitive psyche.

It's always difficult to part ways with the crowd. When you're standing in the spotlight with a check in hand, it only gets tougher.

• Ignorance about the Nonprofit Sector

Some people think of the nonprofit sector as work-lite, an escape from the serious business of everyday getting and spending. They imagine that the sector is staffed by do-gooding paraprofessionals whose activities rank as largely recreational. It goes without saying that such opinions spring from the uninformed and uninitiated. Anybody who has seriously devoted time, effort, and money to righting a wrong, building an institution, or sustaining a necessary public service understands only too well the incessant demands placed on skilled professionals.

Alas, there also exists a small minority that associates nonprofits with scandal and scams. In truth, the few high-profile examples of malfeasance in the nonprofit sector adhere to our collective memory with corrosive tenacity. Think of the long shelf life of the United Way's scandal in the 1990s, when the charity's embezzler-in-chief was convicted of looting donations to underwrite what *Forbes* summed up as "an extravagant and lurid lifestyle." A good excuse not to give? Perhaps, if you're looking for one. But this late-twentieth-century disgrace couldn't be less representative of the sector as a whole. And to be fair, how many of us have closed our bank accounts and cancelled insurance policies following Wall Street's misconduct and the subsequent financial meltdown of 2008? In the nonprofit realm, a little larceny goes a long way towards disenchanting donors.

• Difficulty of Decision Making

Given all the urgent causes and excellent organizations striving to prod the world into better shape, it's damn hard to decide where to place your bet. In foundations, we have established criteria—presumably forged, vetted, and regularly reviewed by a board. We can consult the metrics and formulas that have penetrated philanthropy, perhaps to a fault. We can rely on senior program officers, staff at other institutions, and several lifetimes of amalgamated experience within the realm of organized grantmaking.

Individual giving is naked philanthropy. Donors don't generally embrace the procedures and protocols that foundations employ to insulate themselves, for good and ill, from grantseekers. As a result, we may grow frightened of each knock on the door, assuming every encounter will inevitably include a covert fundraising agenda. Or we become paralyzed, unable to make any decision for dread of picking a bad one. It's a sad truth that even middling wealth can sometimes narrow our horizons, rather than gallantly expanding them. Consider poor King Midas, who turned to gold everything he touched—and then starved to death for want of a slice of apple or bread that wasn't glittering.

For other donors, the prospect of bolder giving turns up the heat on longstanding personal fears.

Who am I to break ranks?

Am I smart enough to take this chance?

What happens when word gets out and everybody wants a piece of me?

Of course, you can always adopt an air of high dudgeon, blithely ignoring all requests and isolating yourself from any encounter you can't control. But who wants to go through life in such a dull, desiccated, and frightened fashion?

Four Ways to Give More Courageously (In Ascending Order of Difficulty)

"After I started giving more prominently," confided one donor, "people began to ask me for advice. I spoke for some time with a man who had quite a lot of money to give, and then months later, I ran into him and asked what he had decided to do. 'I did what you suggested,' he said. 'I gave almost everything to my alma mater's endowment.' And I thought: 'Oh, my god. Did I do that?' That wasn't at all my intention. I thought we had been talking about being just a bit bolder in how you spread your money around. Giving away a substantial sum to an Ivy League college with a huge endowment is the last thing I would have recommended.

"But I also realized that I had been speaking all the time about giving principles. *Abstractions.* And that probably isn't the right way to approach an inexperienced donor. Most of us want direction. We're looking for concrete steps we can take immediately."

In this spirit, here are four rock-hard ways to move down the path of courageous giving:

1. Jump in first.

For most projects, the first donation is the hardest to secure. Skepticism can swamp even the best proposals as potential funders ask themselves:

- Have we just been handed a brilliant idea or a pipe dream?

- Are the people running this show the next wave of leaders or mere beginners who will skulk away at the first sign of trouble?

- Should we take a chance with a promising new organization or stick with the old dependables?

Usually, the hold-on-to-your-wallet approach wins out.

It isn't just a matter of sorting through the latest batch of good ideas and seizing upon the best. Grantmakers of all sizes and persuasions are also motivated by fear.

Nobody wants to climb out on a limb to support an unknown organization or project and then watch it get sawed off by unanticipated events. It's painful and humiliating.

It's also one of the reasons why I think the notion of "venture philanthropy" doesn't carry much weight. Of course, the term is borrowed from venture capitalism—the strategy in which investors pour money into a myriad of business enterprises in hopes that one will click. In search of a winner that can pay back the losses, and *much* more, venture capitalists blaze through vast sums. Consecutive failure is the price of eventual success. The timid need not apply.

In philanthropy, our achievements with one grant can't offset another's collapse. Each endeavor has to be judged on its own. An unambiguous victory in, say, protecting coastal wetlands can't begin to compensate for a string of faltering grants aimed at school reform.

This helps explain why philanthropy tends to be so conservative in its approach. Donors balk at risk taking due to an unspoken and usually unconscious aspiration to limit their losses, liability, and potential embarrassment. (Even though, as we've said, usually nobody is looking…) This reserve—dare I call it fear?—makes the first grant or donation both crucial and exceedingly difficult to obtain.

I urge an opposite approach.

When faced with a promising project, strong leadership, and a genuine need, try rustling up your courage to be the first to fund.

"Our donors took pride in being first to support Alaska's indigenous people when drilling in the arctic became an issue," said an advisor to a group of small family funds. "The tribal members lived way out in the middle of nowhere, without computers or access to the media. They didn't know the decision makers or key political figures. They needed help to make their case about the region's importance and fragility to these people who never journey out to the arctic. Our jumping in first made it safe for larger foundations, who were initially loathe to take a step in what everybody knew would be a controversial issue. But once they saw that we were willing to stick our necks out, they found it much easier."

Credibility is the gift that keeps giving. Sometimes the fact that you have supported a cause can be as important as the gift itself.

"Nonprofits have told us, 'You don't even need to give us money,'" said Shirley Fredricks, vice president of the Lawrence Welk Family Foundation. "Just let us use your name."

A case in point. When the Welk Family Foundation wanted to throw its support behind the Cambodian Children's Fund, its directors used their own contacts and reputation to instantly extend the international charity's reach.

"We hosted a dinner with CCF's president and screened films to introduce their work to Los Angeles donors, foundations, and wealth advisors," remembered Shirley. "I invited wealthy donors, advisors, and funders in the Los Angeles region. Many came because of our name. Our guests were the hub of a wheel in many social and professional circles. They left the event and talked about the Cambodian Children's Fund to their peers. And those people who got involved talked in turn about the group to their friends. We didn't give the organization a big grant. It was only $1,500—but it was the most impactful grant our fifty-year-old foundation ever made. And it was given by our junior board. With this money, CCF was able to go to the forty-five poorest families on the garbage dump in Phnom Penh and supply each home with a new tin roof, a clean water receptacle/filter, and twenty pounds of rice."

2. Give significantly.

For many donors, grantmaking follows the path of their children's lives. Gifts go first to the schools, perhaps the local zoo and Little League, the youth orchestra, ballet, and so on. Children lead us into new worlds, and we pay something for the privilege.

When the kids are grown with kids of their own, then we're often ready for something new. That's usually when the prospects arise for giving a greater share. It's also when some funders refocus their gaze from their immediate family to the larger local community.

"I always direct a portion of my big gifts locally," one donor told us. "You can see the effects with your own eyes. To me, it's self-interested giving in the largest and best sense. I look around for little pockets of energy, rather than wait for proposals. I want to *feel* the possibilities. Plus, it launches me into worlds within my own town that I'd otherwise know nothing about. I learn about my city from the people who are doing the hard work that seldom gets celebrated. We're global citizens now, and that's good, but it also means we can lose energy at the local level if we don't watch out."

The wisdom of deferring to local expertise can apply even when the cause is distant from your own home. Following Haiti's devastating 2010 earthquake, many donors directed their pledges to the Clinton Foundation precisely because it had been operating in-country for years. The staff had already established relationships with key local organizations. Unlike many international relief agencies that flooded the airwaves in search of donations, it didn't have to devote time to learning the basics, forging trust, and identifying the leaders amid a battered populace.

"After Hurricane Katrina," another donor told us, "I gave money to a New Orleans–area community foundation. I knew that even if the waters had driven them out of town, they'd be in a better position to know who was on the ground ready to work when they returned to their offices."

Size counts, too.

"We're always trying to be significant in our grants," observed a seasoned donor with extensive experience in the nonprofit world. "Occasionally, our family gives five thousand dollars, but we try to stay closer to the ten-thousand-dollar level. It's hard for nonprofits to build major support. I know that from my own work as a volunteer. You start with one-hundred-dollar donors and it takes a long time for them to become five-hundred-dollar donors. Then it takes just as long for the five-hundred folks to become thousand-dollar donors. You can do a big favor to everybody by stepping in at a significant level as soon as you're sure you want to back the organization over time. It isn't about helping out a program here and there. Significant donors build institutions over the years that the community can depend on. By giving relatively large amounts locally, we're contributing to the quality of life around us in ways that we'll never completely be able to track. Yet that's a good thing. Money has a life of its own. The challenge is getting it to the right places at the right time and in amounts that make a difference."

Of course, five or ten thousand dollars isn't a small sum for most individuals to give. But it's hardly enough to keep an organization afloat or launch a sustainable initiative. Keep in mind that even among staffed foundations, the median grant is only $20,000.

"Novice donors think $20,000 is heck of a lot of money," said a donor who has for years given at this level. "Of course, it feels a lot bigger leaving my checkbook than it does slipping into the nonprofit's bank account. But we can't expect small grants to vanquish great problems. We have to meet them with commensurate resources."

Alas, the challenge in doing so has only grown more formidable in recent years. In a 2009 survey of 986 nonprofit human service agencies nationwide, the Nonprofit Finance Fund found that only 12 percent expected to do better than break even by year's end. A mere 16 percent foresaw being able to cover operating expenses for the next two years. And nearly a third of the agencies confessed that they had less than thirty days of cash on hand, while another third had less than ninety days' worth.

"Taken together," Kathleen Enright, president and CEO of Grantmakers for Effective Organizations, wrote in 2009, "these statistics paint a grim picture. The vast majority of nonprofits will operate at a deficit this year (and potentially next) without the financial reserves to fill the gaps. The majority of nonprofits already were financially vulnerable before the financial crisis, and pressures from all sides are increasing. Government funders are paying more slowly, foundations are retrenching, and demands for basic services are on the rise. The reality is that even the strongest nonprofits are struggling."

All the research tells us that high-performing nonprofits require a substantial cash reserve—say, six months' worth or so. But that's a necessity most groups will never piece together without sizeable and steady donations of unrestricted funds. Today is the time for donors to step up locally and support the organizations they value most with significant gifts of no-strings funding. This kind of support can give able managers the opportunity to catch their breath and plan for the future—instead of responding to wave after wave of fiscal crisis.

One more point about significant giving. If you're going to do it, do it now. Don't wait for your favorite organization's twenty-fifth anniversary or a plaintive call from its beleaguered board chair or the next time your shorted soybean stocks magnificently plummet and trigger an enhanced round of generosity. "Boldness has genius, power and magic in it"—so goes the incantatory line often attributed to Goethe (but actually the words of one W. H. Murray from his 1951 book about mountaineering, *The Scottish Himalayan Expedition*). So allow me to paraphrase: Do it now so that it gets done.

3. Exceed your giving comfort level—everywhere.

"Every time you add a zero to the amount you're giving," said a long-time donor of sizeable gifts, "you feel your heart take a little leap. You have to catch your breath. Until you put a new frame on what you're trying to accomplish, it can shake you. We tell ourselves, 'I'm a hundred-dollar donor.' Or, 'I'm a thousand-dollar donor—but no more!' To imagine yourself giving a larger amount, wherever your current baseline might be, takes a bit of imagination. It also takes guts."

For decades, charitable giving in the United States has held steady at 2 to 3 percent of income. Even our boom years have failed to appreciably raise this level. Meanwhile, the gap between the rich and the poor widens into a chasm not seen since the 1920s as the top 5 percent of Americans by income spend nearly as much on consumer goods as the bottom 80 percent. And still, our culture manufactures ever more "needs." The family car balloons into an SUV, the forty-dollar cell phone morphs into a four-hundred-dollar smart phone, and our perfectly serviceable television sets swell to the size and expense of a living-room wall.

"There's little consistency about what tells people they have enough," said Jason Franklin, executive director of Bolder Giving, a group that encourages individuals to increase the level of their personal donations. "But the truth is that endless spending on goods and good times really isn't all that satisfying. If you spend $800 on a new iPad, you may enjoy it tremendously. But if you give an $800 gift to a nonprofit, I can guarantee that you'll remember the experience of writing that check much longer. Or maybe you go out with friends for drinks and dancing and spend $200 for a fabulous night. Pretty quickly, you'll forget that evening. Give the same amount to a cause you believe in, and you'll vividly remember it. Plus, the very act of contemplating that gift, and then taking action, can change you in ways that you could never anticipate."

As a donor himself, Jason consults his giving plan every August, reviewing where his contributions went the previous year and what effect he wants them to have in the future. After years of steadily increasing his rate of giving, he now dedicates 25 percent of his income to charitable donations.

"Being a donor is a significant part of my identity," he said. "I come from a family of wealth and we had a foundation that I became active in at the age of twenty-two. Still, that question of how much to give personally is a vexing one. People want a percentage. 'You should give 5 percent, or tithe with 10, or give a quarter of your income, or 90 percent of your assets if you're really wealthy.' We almost always feel that we're not giving as much as we should since we can all look around us and see people who have so much less. It's a struggle for each person to figure how much to give, and there are few places where we can frankly explore this question."

With remarkable dispatch, Bolder Giving has in the first three years of its existence become a key resource for people grappling with matters of size. Through conference calls with seasoned high-level givers, excellent publications, and hands-on coaching, the organization provides just the right blend of inspiration and know-how to guide people at all income levels who want to expand their personal philanthropy.

Recently, the Giving Pledge has thrust the question of how much into a conspicuous light. Responding to the challenge posed by Warren Buffett and Bill and Melinda Gates, sixty-nine American billionaires vowed in the Pledge's debut year to leave half of their assets to nonprofit organizations by the end of their lives. To date, that accounts for some $200+ billion, with other donors likely to eventually add their own fortunes to the pile.

"The Pledge has changed the climate," acknowledged Jason. "Before, people may have thought our call to increase personal giving seemed too radical, outrageous, or odd. Now the idea isn't as scary. It sounds feasible.

Big dollars capture the imagination and get the rest of us thinking about what's possible for *us* to do."

Giving a greater amount can also set an example that ripples through society with unanticipated consequences. In 2010, Bolder Giving got a call from the Gates Foundation from out of the blue, saying that they wanted to fund Bolder Giving to help the organization "go to scale." Bolder Giving carries a companion message to the Giving Pledge—that you don't have to be a billionaire to give big—and has been credited as part of the inspiration for launching the Giving Pledge.

4. Make change.

Most charitable giving fails to address the conditions of poverty, either at home or abroad. According to a 2009 study by the National Committee for Responsive Philanthropy, only one out of every three foundation grant dollars benefits "lower-income communities, communities of color, and other marginalized groups, broadly defined." Other estimates put the funds directly intended to help alleviate poverty at a scant 10 percent. These figures remain controversial, but to me the thrust of the argument is unassailable. Most of us give too little and too infrequently to causes, organizations, and individuals whose animating passion is the eradication of want, suffering, and injustice.

Why does giving frequently (even usually) miss the mark when it comes to transforming a world full of hurt and need? To my mind, it starts with our wobbly aims. Nonprofit enterprise—the destination of most giving—remains a vast and varied universe with voluntary organizations dedicated to the realization of virtually every imaginable goal. "Wherever at the head of some new undertaking you see the government in France, or a man of rank in England," Alexis de Tocqueville famously pronounced in the 1830s, "in the United States you will be sure to find an association." All that has changed in nearly two hundred years is the size of our national effort. In 2009, the Urban Institute's National Center for Charitable Statistics counted 1,581,111 nonprofits in operation, an increase of 31.5 percent over the previous ten years. No wonder donors get lost—even those who passionately want their contributions to aid the most needy and neglected.

But we also have to acknowledge the self-serving quality of some philanthropy. As Robert Reich wrote in a much-argued-over blog post in 2007, a sizeable portion of our nation's charitable donations—"especially from the wealthy, who have the most to donate"—are really "investments in the lifestyles the wealthy already enjoy and want their children to have too. They're also investments in prestige—especially if they result in the family name being engraved on the new wing of an art museum or symphony hall."

Now, I happen to believe that the arts remain an essential constituent of civilization. We abandon their practice and appreciation at our peril. Moreover, contributions to the arts can generate a plethora of practical benefits in terms of education and economic development. (More on this subject in chapter seven.) Nevertheless, I do accept the premise that there's a hierarchy in giving; some things are more important than others. If we tell ourselves that we're truly concerned with the material conditions of our fellow humans—with millions underfed worldwide, billions dirt poor—then at least some of our giving should be aimed accordingly.

What does grantmaking directed at changing the conditions of poverty look like? In foundation circles, we frequently talk about the choice of working downstream, where problems manifest themselves publicly, or upstream, where conditions first cause the problems to arise. Both approaches have merit, particularly when they're bound together to simultaneously alleviate symptoms and neutralize root causes.

Aaron Dorfman, executive director of the National Committee for Responsive Philanthropy (NCRP), summed it up nicely in an op-ed in the *Baltimore Sun*. "A foundation concerned with homelessness," he wrote, "might choose to make a $250,000 grant to a homeless shelter to provide food and shelter for a few hundred people. But if that same foundation instead or in addition gives a $250,000 grant to a nonprofit advocating with or on behalf of homeless people, the grant offers the potential to help leverage millions of dollars in government funding for affordable housing programs, thereby assisting thousands permanently instead of hundreds temporarily."

We need to see more giving at every level to organizations that help the poor to organize in their own interests, advocate for fair and just public policies, and help frame the social and economic inequities of our society and our world in ways that ordinary people can comprehend and engage with. There's compelling evidence that this kind of funding can reap considerable results.

In a study of twenty nonprofit organizations in Idaho, Montana, Oregon, and Washington conducting policy advocacy, community organizing, and civic engagement activities, the NCRP documented substantial returns on the funders' investments. For every dollar donated in program support, the nonprofits garnered an additional $150 in benefits to their communities. In addition, the groups achieved benefits for the underserved that simply can't be monetized—including civil rights protections, promotion of fair immigration policies, and hedges against environmental degradation. Collectively, the groups trained more than 11,000 leaders, grew their memberships by 98,000 individuals, registered more than 71,900 voters, and turned out 417,000 people at public actions.

That doesn't mean you have to abandon all your longstanding giving traditions in favor of some newly kindled activist zeal. (Sometimes addressing root causes is crucial. Other times, the symptoms prove so severe that they require immediate attention.) Still, most funders should at least consider diversifying their philanthropic portfolio. Take a brave and sober look at your annual gifts and ask yourself which ones not only do good work but also give back to you and your family in terms of recognition, prestige, and everyday use. Then include some contributions that speak not at all to *your* self-interest but to the interest of the poor. Pay attention to funding fashions and cycles. Currently, we see foundations staking out an interest in programs dedicated to children, while neglecting older poor people who are at the ends of their lives. In five years, the emphases will probably change. Your giving can plug some of the holes. Or mix your portfolio in terms of predictable results. Keep funding your stalwarts, the groups you can depend on doing good work. But now and then take a flyer on some promising project whose outcome is far from guaranteed.

Finally, give to political campaigns. Support outstanding candidates. Fund important legislative initiatives—or throw your money in the path of wrongheaded juggernauts. No, this kind of giving is not a charitable donation. It's not deductible. But in our democracy, it's imperative that we stand up for what we believe in the public arena and then put our money where our mouths are—as well as our hearts.

All Power to the Imagination:
The Contagious Quality of Distinctly Not-Dull Giving

Beyond the fundamentals of how much and where to give, there's another question that by its nature can never finally be answered. It's a matter that should prod, vex, and motivate every thoughtful donor:

How might I use my money in more imaginative, original, and inspiring ways?

I'm not arguing here for gimmickry. Just because something hasn't been tried before doesn't mean it's the next best candidate for support. But I do feel that philanthropy in all its forms—from the mahogany-encrusted suites of the nation's megafoundations to the most modest levels of personal giving—too often lacks invention. It favors familiarity over verve. It fails to inspire.

We give in the ways that everybody else gives because that's the way giving has always been done. Philanthropy chases its own tail. In the blur, opportunities get lost.

My friend Bill Somerville is an exception. He wakes up each morning with his imagination percolating, eager to fashion some creative new response to the problems of poverty and inequity that have bedeviled us for ages. As the president of Philanthropic Ventures Foundation, he pioneered "Teachers' Fax Grants" (subsequently reliant on email) whereby public school teachers submitted a single-page request for support of a discrete classroom project—and received as much as $500 to cover the costs by the next day's mail.

On another occasion, Bill responded to a donor's request that his foundation address the plight of poor working women by giving a select number the opportunity to "take a paid day off"—a satisfaction familiar among America's middle class but unknown to millions of working poor. After receiving nominations from social workers, school principals, and clergy members Bill had worked closely with in the past, he dispatched checks of $200 through his intermediaries with instructions to "please take the time to rejuvenate yourself in body, mind, and spirit." One woman treated her sister to lunch—something she hadn't been able to afford for years. Then they strolled along the beach for the remainder of the afternoon. Another went to the movies by herself. Several spent half the day in the beauty parlor, spiffing up their nails and hairdos. All had to be coaxed into using the money for their own small pleasures rather than devoting it to their children, which their instincts first dictated.

Now, Bill will readily admit that this inventive and, I imagine, unprecedented use of discretionary funds did nothing to confront the structural conditions that had mired these women in poverty. Still, there's no question that the gesture—no, more than a gesture: an embrace of common humanity!—touched the recipients' hearts, soothed their souls, and, as several proclaimed, offered encouragement to go on. One recipient spoke to Bill about her astonishment at being "appreciated." Another told him that the day off marked the first time in her life she had "ever been given anything."

I welcome the audaciousness of this kind of giving. I'm inspired by the boldness of reaching out with the frank aspiration to ease another person's pain. It's philanthropy out of the mainstream, and perhaps nobody will ever do it again. Nevertheless, I also subscribe to Martin Luther King's dictum that the philanthropist should never "overlook the circumstances of economic injustice which make philanthropy necessary."

What, then, should we do when faced with the ubiquity of need, the ever-presence of suffering? How do we move beyond the symptoms to also treat the causes? Where do we begin?

We begin with our imaginations, aiming to inspire even better ideas.

Observers may disagree with your tactics and strategy, even your motives. But if you fire their imaginations, you may inspire them to storm the ramparts in their own fashion, according to their own visions and values.

The Secret Society for Creative Philanthropy reflects this faith in the contagious quality of imaginative giving. Founded in 2006 by writer Courtney Martin, the Society's web banner neatly frames a fresh conception of the donor's role:

"So you're a human being with an imagination and something to give? Well done. You've met all the requirements for becoming a creative philanthropist. The next step is to give genuinely and joyfully. And remember we're watching. (By the way, you look great today!)"

Courtney breathed life into the not-so-Secret Society (SSCP boasts a vivid web presence and has chapters in New York, San Francisco, Boston, Minneapolis, and Athens, Georgia, with others forming in Seattle, Maui, Krakow, Houston, Vancouver, Los Angeles, and beyond) after receiving a startlingly large book advance. "It was a Cinderella experience," she recalled. "Suddenly, I had money—for the first time in my life. And it was a bit alienating. My friends didn't want to talk about my angst over giving money away. So I knew that I had to take action." Relying on the spark that comes from the creative friction of many hands, Courtney tapped ten thoughtful friends, gave them each $100, and urged them to give it away smartly. "Just having that $100 in your pocket raises questions," she said. "Who am I responsible for? Who is a stranger? What can $100 buy? People answered those questions in both creative and conventional ways." Ultimately, their funding decisions were made public not in an annual report or press conference but at a dance party captured on video and stashed on YouTube. Since then, other people—including the previous years' donors—have contributed additional funds to the cause in a kind of "reverse pyramid scheme," unleashing waves of new "agents" pursuing their own giving opportunities, with the results continuing to be celebrated with the usual big dance party. The Society's agents have purchased a video camera for a public high school, published the writing of children tutored by a literacy nonprofit, supported agencies working in postearthquake Haiti, handed out free umbrellas in the rain, stashed $20 bills in the Young Adult section of the Brooklyn Library ("as a bonus for kids checking out *The Catcher in the Rye*, or whatever they've been assigned at school"), and deferred to the wisdom of crowds on Twitter, where a recommendation to donate to an abortion-rights group in Texas was accompanied by a matching $100 gift.

But the Society's biggest achievement has been the highly public, antic manner in which its activists have welded together an amalgam of personal responsibility and creative thinking, thereby capturing the attention of people who never pictured themselves as philanthropists. Despite the small size of their contributions, the agents take seriously the injunction to give with spontaneity and zest. Everyone recognizes that these gifts aren't going to transform the world. But the insistence that we all can think a little longer and harder—and sometimes a little odder—about how and where we give deserves to spread wide and far.

Retooling Familiar Strategies to Fit Today's Needs

If you're not prepared to leap into the more theatrical forms of philanthropy, there are still plenty of ways to nudge the familiar into something fresh and serviceable.

Take, for example, that esteemed chestnut of so many donors, the scholarship.

I'm not referring to a conventional donation to your alma mater—be it Harvard with its endowment bulging at $27 billion or a more sleekly supported four-year institution. Rather, I'm talking about scholarships destined for the students usually left out of the competition: enrollees of every age and background at your local community college.

Community colleges rank as one of our most important and most neglected public resources. In many places, they're filled with the students who will shape the futures of their states: immigrants, kids from the working class, veterans returning from Iraq and Afghanistan, older workers who must retrain to keep up with globalized job demands. These typically underfunded institutions are the first and last resort for students from less privileged backgrounds struggling to acquire the training they need to ascend to the next rung on the economic ladder.

Community colleges serve as gateways to the trades. They provide technical training in booming fields such as health care and computer technology (with jobs waiting on the other side). They give many students from ailing public schools a second chance to excel by honing their basic skills, so they might then move along to a public university. Unfortunately, community colleges have also been hit hard by the state funding crisis, as costs escalate in tandem with those in beleaguered four-year schools. The crucial difference is that community colleges serve the students who can least afford another bump in fees and tuition, and who have less access to reasonably priced loans.

"They're places where a little can go a long way," emphasized Linda Collins, executive director of the Career Ladders Project, which strives to improve career training for underserved populations. "Right now, we have employers with skills shortages that must be filled if they're to stay in business and grow. We also have an increasingly diverse population with large numbers of people left out of the economy. Over the long run, that's an unsustainable situation. Community colleges are uniquely situated to deal with needs of both employers and future workers. There are lots of opportunities now emerging for donors. You can put money into the hands of students who can't afford the books, tools, and equipment they need to continue their education. Well-paid, family-sustaining jobs that give people a toehold in the regional economy—those are the kinds of programs I'd invest in."

Aid to community colleges can take a variety of forms. A donor might:

- buy equipment directly and give it to an outstanding program,
- establish a scholarship for students entering a field with high employment potential, such as clean energy technology or nursing,
- set up a challenge grant to encourage a community college's operating foundation to fundraise locally for matching gifts, or
- partner with a community organization already working with new students so they have the skills and support network to remain in college.

Of course, the quality of instructional programs, management, and governance varies among community college districts. But even within the most disorganized districts, donors still have found ways to make certain their gifts reach the students who can benefit most. In a building trades program bolstered by English language–learning tutorials and leading to high-wage jobs upon graduation, donors have bypassed an unreliable administrative apparatus to provide supplies and equipment directly to the instructor. In an automotive repair program, donors have helped students purchase their own tools—with each grant recipient taking responsibility for one-third of the cost, thereby ensuring their sense of ownership and solidifying their commitment to their future career.

"It's hard for donors to find the front door," acknowledged a former community college instructor. "How do you get to the right people who will respond positively to an imaginative gift? How do you steer your money through the bureaucracy? It's different in every district."

Donors keen to work with their local community colleges might start by making an appointment with the district's director of development. Or you can consult the vice president of instruction, who runs academic side of the house. Or the dean who works under the school's vice president. Or a department chair known for her commitment and moxie. Or you might seek out an experienced education reporter in the local press who knows the inside scoop about your district's most visionary teachers and most reliable administrators. In every case, you'll be searching for that ideal collaborator: an individual in a position of power with vision and energy.

Community colleges are just one of many cash-strapped public institutions that donors might creatively aid. In your own area, it may be your park district that needs assistance, or your community mental health clinics. In fact, you're a fortunate individual if your community *isn't* facing dire cutbacks in multiple essential services. The fiscal outlook for cities and states can't be called rosy these days. But that means donors with imagination and initiative are more important than ever.

A Final Thought about Failure

Sometimes failure is the best medicine, if you're willing to take it.

If you're a courageous and imaginative donor, you will occasionally fall on your face. That's the price of boldness. Pick yourself up. Figure out what went wrong. Recalibrate your giving strategy and try again.

If you fail to do so, you're wasting the most precious capital of personal philanthropy: its freedom. As an individual donor, you have few, if any restraints.

Take advantage of this freedom. It's rare, both in public and private life. Recognize that your giving can be risk capital, unfettered by burdensome oversight, free of most regulations, unseen by almost everybody in the world except you.

Finally, you'll be the only one to know if you've combined sufficient ambition, vision, good judgment, and courage to take the kind of risks philanthropy demands.

5

The Never-Ending Education of a Donor

Principle #5 *Learn from others.*

"When I started working with my family's philanthropy," recalled Radha Stern, "I knew that I had a lot to learn. The question was where to start. I sent away for a booklet outlining philanthropy basics, but it turned out to be a pitch from a bank looking for customers. I called a technical assistance organization for nonprofits and said, 'I'm trying to figure out how to give away money. Can you help me?' I later learned that the staff had a twenty-dollar bet riding as to whether I was a kook. Finally, a friend told me, 'You have to meet my cousin Eddie.' I thought, 'The last thing I need is to meet somebody's cousin Eddie."

But cousin Eddie turned out to be Ed Nathan, one of the nation's most innovative grantmakers, who served as the executive director of the Zellerbach Family Foundation for more than thirty years.

"He opened doors for me," said Radha. "Ed saw that I was a serious student, and that I wanted to learn as much as I could. He introduced me to Adele Corvin, Bruce Sievers, Claude Rosenberg—all these leaders in Bay Area philanthropy. I needed to fund over a million dollars in five counties within a few months with my family's charitable lead trusts. But we didn't even have guidelines. Thankfully, I found an openness among all of these people to somebody young and hungry to do good in the world. If I had any question, no matter how small, I'd ask."

Sometimes the questions revolved around the minutiae of foundation philanthropy. "Like who pays for lunch?" remembered Radha. "I had worked for years in the grocery industry, and there you buy lunch one week, your colleague buys next. So what about philanthropy? 'Radha,' Ed told me, 'the funder *always* buys.'"

More often, counsel involved more complex matters of planning, research, collaborating with other funders, and leveraging smaller gifts into greater impact. As important, Radha's tutors spoke frankly about the emotional life of giving:

"One of the best things anybody told me was that your gut is right most of the time. Over the years, that turned out to be true. But it was very helpful to hear those words spoken early on by somebody I respected. I got confirmation that I was on the right track."

Today Radha stands out as a savvy, committed donor—someone whose counsel others new to giving now routinely seek. Yet even with her own philanthropic practice firmly established, she still maintains relationships with the people who originally served as her mentors.

"It's not just the information at the beginning of your efforts that's crucial," she emphasized. "What's equally important is the relationships you build that continue to nurture and educate you. Networks like to be used. I treasure the people who've helped me over the years, and I hope they feel treasured."

Radha speaks wisely. Over the decades, I've received many calls at the Packard Foundation from people new to philanthropy, and the ones that I feel best about invariably include a moment when the caller confesses that she's worried about not doing a good job. I reply that *I'd* be worried if she wasn't worried—and then something between us usually clicks. I know that I am speaking with an eager learner who can put our mutual time to good use. And while it's true that most experienced donors enjoy helping others to master their craft, I am sorry to say that there remains a reluctance among people new to the field to seek out guidance and counsel.

"Donors often fail to think of themselves as investors," explained Radha. "They don't delve into the subject in the way they might with a business venture. When I started out, I attended every course and training I could find about how the nonprofit sector works. I took classes in the basics of management and governance. I got insight into the voluntary sector and learned how it differs from the business world. I studied fundraising, grant writing, and fiscal planning from the agency perspective. For a long time, I'd go on thirty site visits each year. That just made sense to me because when I was working in the food business, I used to visit ten to fifteen groceries each day. 'You have the best job in the world,' people would tell me. 'Giving away money. It's so easy.' Well, it's not. I want to make investments in things that will grow. I also love learning something new, and the entire project of immersing myself in philanthropy has made me feel like a kid in candy store."

Into the Issues

People new to philanthropy are often urged to volunteer at one or more nonprofit organizations. I think that's sound advice. At the Packard Foundation, our staff spend a week each year volunteering at the nonprofit of their choice. Everybody benefits—probably the foundation most of all, since it keeps our staff, almost all nonprofit veterans, in touch with current issues and alive to the pressures of daily life in the sector.

Volunteering deepens your understanding of issues, organizations, needs, and strategies. It makes palpable the problems you might otherwise consign to the realm of theory, and opens your eyes to the constant struggle that characterizes the voluntary sector. No substitute exists for getting your hands dirty alongside your nonprofit partners.

After all, they're the experts. As donors, we merely put needed resources at the disposal of the managers, staff, and volunteers who do the real work. We get into trouble when we assume that our own professional experience—be it making a mint in commercial real estate, exploring the genome, or managing the family portfolio—somehow qualifies us to plunge blindly into a large and important sector of American society whose sense and sensibility remains unfamiliar. (If you've spent most of your career in business or government, you'll find differences in the nonprofit world that will amaze you.) Indeed, it's one of the cardinal sins of philanthropy to don the mantle of presumptive expertise and dictate to prospective grant recipients what their goals should be and how their programs should operate. We're simply not close enough to the problems our nonprofit partners are trying to solve day after day.

That's not to say we can't learn about the *issues*. Health care. Education. The environment. Public policy and international development. There's no lack of fascinating, complicated realms to explore. And the better part of our education is going to come from honest and intimate acquaintance with nonprofit professionals slogging away in the trenches.

That's something Elizabeth Wilcox understands. As the former advisor to a group of small foundations concerned with the plight of low-wage workers, she invested prodigious amounts of time researching issues and then disseminating her knowledge among the foundations' trustees.

"I'm proud of the sweat equity that made our meetings useful," she acknowledged. "Say we'd get a proposal about launching a living wage campaign for janitors in Los Angeles. I'd ask, 'Where else has this kind of plan been enacted? How did it win support, and how has it been working out so far? What kind of coalitions backed it, who opposed it, and what were the arguments on all sides?' Then I'd go to L.A. and meet with the

nonprofit groups in the coalition, including organizers working with janitors, day laborers, and garment workers fighting sweatshops. I'd talk with
the janitors themselves. I might tag on a visit to an environmental group
looking at freshwater resources because that was one of our funders' other
interests. I wanted to take full advantage of being in the neighborhood
and out of my office. When I finally got home, I'd dig up like-minded
funders with experience supporting similar drives and interview the program officers, who knew more than I did. I'd talk with organizers from
our own town who had some perspective on how the work was faring five
hundred miles away. In the end, I could bring to our funders all that I had
learned, and I could lead a discussion that was based on fact, experience,
and analysis. This was a wonderful part of my job. I had no choice but to
keep learning about the issues that interested me most from the people
who were closest to the work."

Sometimes Elizabeth introduced the people she was meeting out in
the field into the foundation conference room. That way her donors could
hear directly about projects in process, while acquiring a visceral sense of
the individuals most intimately engaged.

"I'd bring in youth leaders from high schools organizing in Sacra-
mento to protect education funding, or environmental activists restoring
salmon in the local creeks. They could communicate directly with our
donors in ways I couldn't replicate. There's an energy that takes over the
room in these situations. You can't manipulate or fake it—you can only
create the conditions that allow it to happen. Timing also comes into the
picture. These conversations are more likely to occur when donors aren't
feeling the pressure of voting on the docket. Neither should they feel like
they're being pitched by the speakers. Donors need a safe space without
the 'Big Ask' hovering over their heads. They need time and room to learn."

I think that's an important insight. Of course, you don't want to
overwhelm your trustees with a parade of speakers, who'll only inspire

confusion—or just a single speaker, who will inevitably end up advocating for his own interests. Keep the program to four or five presenters who can expand and challenge your collective worldview.

There's always a bit of pain involved with learning. Sure, it's a *good* pain—sometimes akin to your leg muscles burning at the conclusion of a long day's challenging hike. But it's also a pain we have to persistently court and learn to endure, since we almost always know less than we need about any given issue. Prying ourselves open to absorb a bit more information whenever opportunity allows becomes a habit, despite the sting.

Interestingly, when we acknowledge the limits of our knowledge, we make it easier for nonprofits to be frank about their own struggles. Staff will feel that they don't have to limit their communication with you to the latest triumph or lucky break. With time and trust, you'll also hear about the troubles, disappointments, mistakes, defeats. This is crucial, since failure often proves a more able tutor than success. In the best of possible worlds, you and the organizations you support will edge ever closer towards mutual honesty about your respective growing pains. You'll assist one another in your shared quest for skill and understanding.

Teaching One Another

Four times each year, members of the Global Sojourns Giving Circle convene remotely via telephone conference call, trading information about projects they fund in Zambia and South Africa. Peter Macy, who heads up the effort in partnership with his wife, Priscilla, had just returned from Livingstone, Zambia, where the Global Sojourns Giving Circle helped sponsor a career workshop for adolescent girls.

There was plenty to talk about…

Twenty-two girls had attended the career workshop. A counselor spoke to them about the importance of continuing their education, while acknowledging the problems they all faced: endless chores, noise, no place to study at home. Most of all, she stressed the determination required to rise above the meager expectations placed upon even the brightest, most motivated young women in their community.

"It was wonderful," said Peter, addressing fourteen members of the giving circle who were listening from their homes in Washington, California, Colorado, Oregon, and the District of Columbia. "The girls had their hands up constantly. These were the best and brightest, and they got their questions answered and their comments heard. The guidance counselors said that they had nothing like this to offer back in their own schools."

Which led to the project's next step, also supported by the Global Sojourns Giving Circle: a far more ambitious career day that brought together eighty-five local girls and their town's professional women— including a doctor, lawyer, and an accountant who braved the 111-degree heat to get their message across.

"These women didn't just stress their accomplishments," explained Peter. "They also spoke of their severe struggles as girls. They said, 'You, too, can make it.' They described how their vision and dedication moved them forward. They covered all the steps, one by one, that delivered them to their goals. *Boom*, up shot all these hands! Girls pining for information, longing get their questions answered. Smart, passionate questions."

At the end of the reports, the giving circle members posed a number of questions. Why the focus on girls? (All the statistics say it pays off in reducing AIDS risk and pregnancy, and has a positive influence on future household economics.) How does the work compare to other regional efforts? (A GSGC member who had been a Peace Corps volunteer enthused that focusing on career information for girls was the best project she'd been involved with during her time in Zambia.) What language did participants speak at the sessions? (Local people know several languages, but English served as the common tongue.) Plans were then discussed for the coming year: the possibility of forming career clubs for girls; the need to train teachers to work with clubs; the aim of reaching three hundred girls at the next career day.

By the hour's end, everybody participating in the giving circle's conference call knew much more about what their donations were helping to accomplish. Plus, they had an intimate view of developments in faraway Africa from trusted individuals who had recently been there.

"It's amazing the impact this group has had," said Priscilla. "And all on a shoestring." In their first year, members of the Global Sojourns Giving Circle contributed $14,000 to aid projects in Africa. The following year, the sum grew to $22,000. "We're never going to be a huge organization," Priscilla emphasized. "But we don't need to be to have an effect."

Giving circles represent a growth area in philanthropy. Typically, the circles bring together a dozen or so individuals who study the issues and then pool their resources, enabling the group to make larger, better-informed contributions than any single household might undertake. In recent years, giving circles have poured millions of dollars into useful projects in their local communities—or, like the Global Sojourns Giving Circle, in places far from home. Due to their autonomy and decentralized nature, it's difficult to specify exactly how many giving circles exist nationwide. Recently, the Forum of Regional Associations of Grantmakers identified some four hundred groups with more than twelve thousand donors giving close to $100 million during the course of their giving circles' existence. But the study also estimated that four or five times as many giving circles may be operating under the radar.

By all indications, giving circles prompt donors to plan strategically, give larger amounts of money, and participate more thoroughly in community life. In the long run, they also provide participants with the means of becoming more effective philanthropists, often without leaving their neighborhoods.

Cooperative learning is etched into the DNA of giving circles. At their best, the informed conversation encourages curiosity and clarity, rejecting both received notions about the state of the world and fuzzy thinking about philanthropic methods. Some giving circles establish ambitious research goals. Members may comb their own communities for several months to collect facts and figures about homelessness or scour the web for the best investments in health care in Central Asia or South America. The social aspect is also important. Participants frequently characterize their activities as "parties with a purpose," with monthly potlucks serving as the glue that holds the membership together. Whatever the structure or protocols, the giving circle is proving to growing numbers of individuals to be a powerful means of putting their money to good use—while becoming wiser about our world and the prospects for improving it.

Going Deeper

Sometimes giving circles can even provide the inspiration for rigorous, structured study—the kind of investigation that few individuals would undertake on their own.

Consider, for example, Linda Dee, a longtime Global Sojourns Giving Circle member with an abiding interest in Africa. After returning a few years ago from Mozambique, Linda began thinking about the continent's common tribulations, her own experience as a donor, and her growing conviction that philanthropy must have as great an impact as possible.

"I'd been to Africa before," said Linda, "but I never saw that kind of poverty. It moved me. I wanted to do something. But I wanted that something to be effective."

Back home in Denver, she contacted a friend with similar interests. They talked about the complexity of Africa's problems, while also acknowledging how little they knew about possible solutions. Gamely, they decided to start a book club focusing on development issues. Another friend introduced them to Dr. Jean Scandlyn, an anthropology professor specializing in global health at the University of Colorado Denver, and she agreed to lead the group. Word spread, and soon twenty women were chipping in one hundred dollars apiece for a year's worth of facilitated house meetings, home study, and ultimately, a radical re-envisioning of what they could do to improve prospects for the world's poor.

"Some of us had been to Africa and wanted to learn more," recalled Linda. "Others hoped to go someday. We came from social work, business, education, but we didn't really know each other personally. After several months in an intimate home setting, talking over issues that were literally about life and death, all that changed."

Jean assembled a challenging reading list drawing from a variety of perspectives. The group started their reading with David Bornstein's *How to Change the World*, an influential primer on social entrepreneurship, and then followed up with Tracy Kidder's account of Dr. Paul Farmer's work in Haiti, *Mountains Beyond Mountains*. Each monthly session focused on a theme: women, health and social justice, food and hunger, ecotourism, politics.

"Jean had us read about the Nobel Prize winner Muhammad Yunus and the Grameen Bank in Bangladesh, which lends small amounts of money to the poor to start up businesses," said Linda. "I didn't know much about microfinance and I thought at first that it sounded like nirvana. 'Let's just put all our money into microlending institutions and then everything will be fine!' But the next book we read looked at some of the underlying problems that weren't being discussed yet in the mainstream media." Conversation about the potential of microfinance became more nuanced as book club members learned about the repayment difficulties facing very poor people, the predatory loan practices of for-profit institutions flocking to the emerging market, and the diverse political cultures that shaped the reality of microfinance in Bolivia, India, Rwanda, and Mexico.

"Everybody wanted to go deeper," remembered Jean. "So I included some of the more accessible academic work. We watched films. *Pills Profits*

Protest, a documentary about the movement to bring HIV treatment to the world's poorest and most marginalized communities." The group viewed portions of the six-hour *Rx for Survival* series originally broadcast on PBS, which traced the stories of individual health care workers saving millions of lives across the globe. "Depending on your degree of readiness," acknowledged Jean, "these issues get to your core. I knew that group members wouldn't be writing papers or necessarily reading supplementary materials. The integration of the material would come from our discussions, and that took place at a high level. Any of the participants would have been comfortable in one of my college classes."

"It was fantastic," echoed Linda. "I felt like I'd started a master's degree in international development." In fact, one group member did return to school to pursue a graduate degree, after spending two months in South America volunteering on a project delivering fresh water to rural communities. "By the end, we had ten people on a waiting list who wanted to join us. This coming year, we're planning to start another group."

The Loneliness of the Individual Donor— and How to Cure It

"You need two things to give well and to keep giving," an experienced donor once told me. "Inspiration and support. You're not going to get either one when your philanthropy remains an entirely private matter."

The people who inspire us most profoundly usually reside close at hand. We rely on our families and friends for models of behavior and a sense of the possible. They're also our most common sources of support.

But when you want to strike out in a new direction, and perhaps leave behind some of the habits and assumptions of your upbringing, social class, and circle of acquaintance, it's necessary to reach out to new people.

The head of a small family foundation once told me about her early quest to learn about philanthropy.

"At first," she said, "I attended every training offered by the Council on Foundations and the Southern California Grantmakers. If the workshop was about engineering, I went to it. I just wanted to learn. I had no problem saying, 'I don't know. Help me out.' When you ask, people respond."

But her real education started in the wake of the Los Angeles riots in 1992.

"Many Foundations were asking what they could do. I was chair of the Southern California Grantmakers board and we launched a feasibility study that resulted in the creation of L.A. Urban Funders, with thirty foundations committed to pooling funds to improve neighborhood conditions. This effort spanned twelve years and was the largest, most successful foundation collaborative in our country to date. In L.A., we are still learning and building on the lessons learned. As for me personally, it plunged me into the life of Los Angeles in ways I couldn't have imagined. My son later told me that going on site visits with me during this period was the single most formative experience of his adolescence. It changed my life, too. I couldn't go to another book club or luncheon in the privileged neighborhoods of Brentwood because they seemed so unreal. I realized that I'd rather be spending my time with the immigrant women in East L.A. because they were talking about issues. I came to understand that philanthropy is a graduate course in which you get to constantly re-enroll."

When I was starting out in philanthropy, few options existed for professional development. Of course, I read everything I could get my hands on. But to tell the truth, there wasn't much.

Today, the person who wants to learn about philanthropy faces a very different situation. Every publishing season brings another shower of weighty tomes. (You've got one of the lighter ones in your hands right now.) Meanwhile, there's a near-constant deluge of scholarly articles, opinion pieces, blog posts, scathing critiques, and hopeful suggestions scattered about in print and pixels. You can't read them all. You don't need to try. These days, an immense degree of cogitation is devoted to management theory, world historical analysis, dueling dialectics, and the minutiae of various giving tools—that is, the theory and practice of giving. The *business*.

Which is fine. Up to a point.

But I think a serious donor needs first of all to immerse himself in the nature of the problems he hopes to address. If you're interested in drug treatment, homelessness, or the crisis in public education, then devote study time to an excellent journalistic account of what's happening in our country right now. The authors of the best topical nonfiction spend years investigating their subjects, frequently dispelling conventional wisdom with accurate on-the-ground reporting. Think about Alex Kotlowitz's *There Are No Children Here*, which traces the lives of poor kids growing up in Chicago's housing projects; or Anne Fadiman's remarkable portrait of an immigrant family's clashes with the public health system in *The Spirit Catches You and You Fall Down;* or Lonny Shavelson's groundbreaking work on drug rehabilitation, *Hooked*. Each of these books required total immersion in the subject. As a result, they provide far more insight and context than you could hope to collect on your own. What's more, they're engrossing good reads. You might even experiment with reading two or three accounts of an issue from contrasting points of view—as Jean Scandlyn so deftly encouraged her development book club to do. It's healthy to shake up your thinking now and then, particularly with the subjects that you think you have mastered.

Still, there eventually comes a time when you must put down your book, fold up your journal, click off the computer—and start talking to people. I stress this point because in our incessantly wired world, we tend to overlook human encounters as a deep, verifiable source of understanding.

So where do you begin? How do you separate valuable life lessons from well-meaning rambles? Who's the right individual for you to meet at this moment?

Early in my career, I was fortunate to have friends working at Stanford's development office who provided wise counsel. Over time, I met a number of keen-sighted trustees and program officers employed by the foundation world, both in the Bay Area and beyond. I peppered them all with questions. Whenever I felt besieged by uncertainties, I reached out—at conferences, in foundation hallways, over the phone. I was uniformly treated with generosity and encouragement. Still, I always hungered for more information, contrarian viewpoints, and new directions. Wherever I could locate another wellspring of wisdom and experience, I drank as deeply as my own capacities allowed.

The need for colleagues never ends. I've been working in philanthropy for most of my life now, and I'm probably more attuned today to the counsel and challenges of my peers than I was starting out. In the company of others, we get an opportunity to reexamine our plans and perceptions with fellow givers and determine which are relevant in the calculus of our personal philanthropy. We can make certain that our decision making isn't conducted in a hall of mirrors. We lose some of the loneliness that seldom gets spoken of in philanthropy, and move closer to the shared enterprise that can be the heart of giving.

Today, numerous opportunities exist for the eager student to engage colleagues, teachers, and mentors—and to come alive to the electricity running through a host of networks.

National philanthropy organizations once meant the Council on Foundations. As the former interim president of the Council, I can speak to its prodigious resources for training. Every year, the Council sponsors conferences that provide an ideal introduction for individuals new to philanthropy, with many workshops explicitly devoted to this purpose. But today, the Council hardly stands alone. Throughout the year, excellent educational opportunities are also conducted by the Association of Small Foundations, the National Center for Family Philanthropy, and the Philanthropic Initiative—all of whose activities are worth monitoring through their online presence and mailing lists.

Place-based funders groups provide formal training and access to more experienced peers. Thirty-two regional associations operate throughout the United States, covering all but four states and representing more than four thousand grantmakers. While the obvious place to start is your own region, you should not hesitate to cross state boundaries for events or to make connections with individuals whose work and reputations have ignited your interest. The online Forum of Regional Associations of Grantmakers is the place to begin.

Issue-oriented affinity groups bring together funders with common interests. Like-minded organizations and individuals presently make up thirty-nine affinity groups linked through the Council on Foundations. Some groups form around the populations they serve, such as Grantmakers for Children, Youth and Families; and the Africa Grantmakers' Affinity Group. Others identify by donor, such as Asian Americans/Pacific Islanders in Philanthropy, Emerging Practitioners in Philanthropy, and the Women's Funding Network. The majority are issue based with concentrations in topics such as the arts, environment, AIDS, and civic participation, including many areas that have been historically overlooked and underfunded. The Council of Foundations website provides a complete list and easy means for locating funders in your own interest realm.

Membership groups and training institutes have sprung up around the country with varied approaches to expanding donor knowledge. The Institute for Philanthropy offers intensive training for new donors as well as a specialized course for young people in "Next Generation Philanthropy." The Institute holds workshops worldwide, with the current batch, as I write, taking place in New York, London, and Sierra Leone. Social Venture Partners bills itself as "a network of engaged philanthropists" bringing together "worlds that typically do not overlap: grant making, volunteerism, nonprofit capacity building, and philanthropic education." Training is facilitated through twenty-six partner organizations in the U.S.A., Canada, and Japan. The Global Philanthropists Circle links sixty-five philanthropic families from more than twenty-five countries committed to fighting global poverty and social injustice. GPC staff help members with peer partnerships, regional and issue working groups, foundation contacts and connections to business and multilateral organizations, and individual meetings with key leaders in civil society, government, and the private sector.

Philanthropic advisors include organizations such as the Philanthropic Initiative in Boston, which has for more than twenty years consulted with individuals, families, and foundations "working to realize deep social impact." Rockefeller Philanthropy Advisors similarly consults with wealthy individuals through their offices in New York, Chicago, Los Angeles, and San Francisco. The National Network of Consultants to Grantmakers provides a national database of seasoned consultants organized by region and expertise. On a smaller scale, individual consultants have in recent years established small shops in most metropolitan regions—often with a focus on specialized giving areas, such as peace and justice, social entrepreneurship, and women's organizations.

University offerings in nonprofit management have spread to 292 institutions, including 168 graduate degree programs with nonprofit concentrations. A select few, such as Indiana University, also offer studies in philanthropy. For a current list of academic programs, visit the website of Independent Sector.

Nonprofit technical assistance organizations can provide insight into the workings of the voluntary sector and its challenges in management and governance—an overlooked area for many fledgling students of philanthropy. You might begin your inquiries with some of the nation's leading groups, including: CompassPoint Nonprofit Services in San Francisco, Third Sector New England, the Grassroots Institute for Fundraising Training (GIFT) in Oakland, California (which also publishes the excellent magazine *Grassroots Fundraising Journal)*, or Greenlights for Nonprofit Success in Austin, Texas. Centered in Washington, D.C., Grantmakers for Effective Organizations (GEO) is a national coalition of more than 2,000 individual members representing 350 grantmaking organizations committed to building strong and effective nonprofit organizations. Its staff and members provide a range of trainings, convenings, and helpful publications. Finally, every grantmaker with an eye to understanding the world of grantseekers should acquaint him- or herself with the Foundation Center and its five regional centers in New York, Atlanta, Cleveland, San Francisco, and Washington, D.C. Or turn immediately to the Foundation Center's unmatched bevy of resources on the web.

A Word about Values

During my tenure at the Packard Foundation, our board and staff wrestled with a question essential to all philanthropic endeavors: What do we value most?

I'm not talking about organizations we admired or changes we wanted to make on a programmatic basis. Rather, we stepped back from the nitty-gritty of grantmaking to ask ourselves about the attitudes and actions we aspired to embrace as donors—our ways of being in the world.

It's not an easy conversation to initiate or manage. But we devoted many hours to discussion, rumination, wordsmithing—often finding an abstraction slipping between our fingers just as we were coaxing it into submission with a telling phrase or ringing word.

Finally, we nailed down these five principles:

- **Integrity** The board and staff will be open and honest with one another, the community, and Foundation grantees. We will encourage the highest possible standards of conduct and ethics.

- **Respect for all people** The board and staff, in all of their work on behalf of the Foundation, will show graciousness and respect to all people. The success of the Foundation depends on seeking out and listening to the ideas and advice of others.

- **Belief in individual leadership** The board and staff will provide and promote an environment of trust and flexibility that fosters and rewards the best in ideas and efforts. In grantmaking and other activities of the Foundation, the board and staff will look for those individuals and organizations that are best able to make a contribution in their fields, and then will respect and support their leadership and ideas.

- **Commitment to effectiveness** The board and staff will identify unique and strategic opportunities to make a difference. They will evaluate their effectiveness and change strategies as necessary to achieve a greater effectiveness. The Foundation will take a long-term view and keep a commitment to selected areas that require this.

- **Capacity to think big** The board and staff will initiate and be receptive to ideas in which a large commitment of funds and/or time can make a unique and lasting contribution. The Foundation will operate in a way that ensures flexibility to respond to such opportunities.

I'm not suggesting these values will serve you or your foundation. They're right for us, and we do everything we can to make sure they're driven deeply into our daily operations. Whenever a trustee joins the board or a new staff member is hired, we talk them through the values, trying to link each with a bevy of possible behaviors. (What does integrity mean for a board member being pitched for a grant by an old friend? How can a program officer say no to an applicant with forthright courtesy and respect?) Of course, the real zingers come up when you're faced with competing values—when you have to choose between loyalty and truthfulness, short-term effectiveness versus long-range impact, order or compassion, the fate of the individual or the good of the community.

These kinds of choices come up frequently in philanthropy. We may possess the means to spark change and alleviate suffering, but we don't enjoy unlimited means. We have to make choices. Those choices should be founded on our values.

For me, the institutional values of philanthropy also have to comport with my personal values. That's not always an easy call. So in every decision I make as a funder, I try to apply four standards initially formulated by the Institute for Global Ethics.

1. **The Golden Rule** How would I feel about being on the receiving side of my decision or action?

2. **The Utilitarian Formula** What decision makes probable the greatest good for the greatest number?

3. **The Newspaper Test** How would I feel about seeing my decision splashed across tomorrow's front page?

4. **The Gut Check** Finally, how do I *feel* about my actions?

Coming to grips with your personal and institutional values takes time. There's no one right way to tackle the assignment. Small family foundations and individual donors both can benefit from the use of a consultant to facilitate the conversation. (Or frank talk around the dinner table with friends and family may also get you started down the right road.) The goal is to emerge from the process with two tools in hand:

- a document clearly stating your values as a donor, and

- a habit of consulting your adopted values in plotting your course as a donor.

Growing Into Knowing

Becoming a wise and effective donor can take a lifetime.

It's a journey that will only begin with your initiative. You set the terms, establish the goals, and pursue the contacts. Ultimately, you're the sole person responsible for taking advantage of the embarrassment of riches that makes our education as donors so easy, rewarding, compelling, and absolutely necessary.

And as you learn more, your approach to giving will almost certainly change.

People usually start by giving from the heart. They're full of passion, empathy, and maybe a bit of righteous anger. They see something on TV or on the street that moves them, and they respond. But after some time, impatience and frustration can set in. You give to an organization combating hunger, but years later there are still hungry people. Either you ignore the contradiction, grow frustrated and burned out, or you expand your view to absorb the larger picture. You begin to ask yourself: Why does hunger persist when there's enough food for everybody? What part of the problem is systemic? Who's doing something about the inequities in the system, and how can I help? Philanthropy is always a negotiation between thought and feeling, rational analysis and emotional drive.

Making the transition from well-meaning to effective philanthropy requires a great deal from the donor. You have to start asking uncomfortable questions, sticking your neck out, mixing with people outside your usual frame of reference—and perhaps outside your comfort zone. Most of all, you need to listen hard. If we're lucky, these manifold efforts may reward us with a smattering of knowledge, a few dependable colleagues, and scads more questions than we had when we started out. Experience teaches us how much we have to learn.

6

Getting Real about
Virtual Philanthropy

Principle #6 *Expand your reach with technology.*

For younger donors, the admonition to use technology is like reminding them to put on their shoes when they step out into a storm. They're not going to forget. When it comes to solving problems and delving into new interests, they reach for technology instinctively. When one tool doesn't fit the task, they find another. Or they revise, reinvent, and subsequently send the world spinning in a new direction. A better solution waits around every corner.

For older donors, technology isn't second nature. It's learned. It's incorporated slowly. Gradually adapted. Finally accepted. Sometimes we need a reminder before wandering into heavy weather.

I acknowledge these facts with some chagrin. I'm not just an older donor. I also served as the president of a foundation based on one of the pioneering fortunes of Silicon Valley.

So, yes, technology is frequently in my thoughts, if not quite in my bloodstream. I recognize the changes wrought in philanthropy by the new era of connectivity. After all, philanthropy is about making connections. The age-old tasks of locating good funding investments and then supporting them, keeping track of their progress, and spreading the word about the need to scale up or pare back has grown far easier thanks to tools we now take for granted, along with others just hazily coming into view. Technology is making philanthropy faster, more flexible, highly visible, extremely interesting, and smarter.

But it isn't changing everything.

Before we talk about the promise of our growing connectivity, let's first specify what technology can't do.

Contrary to much ballyhoo and widespread misunderstanding, it can't present you with a no-fuss, effort-free, unbiased, and accurate directory of what's out there worth funding. It can't replace judgment, curiosity, and hours devoted to soul-searching. Technology can kick-start your investigation into promising nonprofits and challenging causes. But it shouldn't conclude it. You can't trade silicon for shoe leather—or self-knowledge.

Take the example of online charity rating services.

In recent years, a growing number of rating services have tried to usher donors through the maze of 1 million-plus tax-exempt organizations to find the "best" ones to support. Until recently, most services have relied on the percentage of "overhead" versus "program" expenditures as the demonstrable key to excellence. Herein lies the problem. Nonprofits wander all over the ledger when it comes to categorizing their expenditures. One organization writes down its executive compensation as overhead, while another divides that cost among programs. The same goes for electric bills, garbage collection, office rental—the full score of organizational incidentals and necessities. Comparisons turn out to be a feast of apples and oranges. What's more, as any entrepreneur (or nonprofit executive) can tell you, "overhead" isn't a code word for waste and rapine. It's the necessary price for getting things done. If you try running a program without budgeting for sufficient salaries, insurance, or training, soon you'll be running your organization into the ground.

To its credit, Charity Navigator, the leading rating service, has taken these criticisms seriously, revamping its system to include categories for accountability and transparency, while working on criteria for that thorniest of issues: results. Based on third-party reviewers wielding standardized queries about effectiveness, the results category will soon carry 50 percent of the new rating's weight. Whatever the final outcome, inevitably there will be debate, dispute, contention, all probably good for philanthropy and the nonprofit sector—thanks in part to the ever-expanding corner of the blogosphere dedicated to discussions of giving.

"Imagine a world," suggested Sean Stannard-Stockton on his excellent blog, *Tactical Philanthropy,* "where Oprah or Bill O'Reilly or CNBC or your local news anchor runs a story on a nonprofit, and when it is time for the hard-hitting question, the host doesn't ask about overhead but instead begins asking questions about the nonprofit's results. That's the world I want to live in. That's the world the Smart Giving movement is working towards. That's the world that's coming."

I hope so. But I have another problem with the rating systems, however they're constructed. I worry about the temptation for donors to rely on them as the first and last step. Instead of opening the discussion about where to give and why—including the incalculable questions What do I care about and What do I want to achieve?—the dependence on sweatless digital selection can bring personal reflection and organizational investigation to a screeching halt. Rating systems may be a good place for some donors to begin. They're a terrible place to remain.

To my mind, technology shouldn't strive so much to pick nonprofit winners and losers as to open doors. Technology is dynamic, not static—it's a beacon, not a hammer. Rather than short-circuiting research and reflection, technology should be facilitating conversation, easing transparency, and extending our philanthropic reach.

And that's just what's happening.

More and Better Conversation about Giving

I recall a time not so many years ago when discussion of philanthropy was pretty much limited to professional philanthropists. Those of us employed as foundation staff got together a few times each year to chew over the usual concerns. Sometimes staff convened regionally, particularly in the cities rife with big fortunes and large foundations. Conversations could be stimulating, challenging, even transformational. But for the most part, philanthropy remained a closed system.

Not so today. New technologies are disseminating insights, experiences, opposing visions, breaking events, and emerging tools among donors of all sizes and persuasions. And it's making philanthropy healthier and more democratic.

The quantity and quality of conversation has never been so extensive or nearly as keen. On practically every occasion when I scroll through the web, I learn something useful, get my worldview challenged, or draw a dash of inspiration from the expanding philanthropic conversation. There's simply too much good stuff being written right now about philanthropy and nonprofit enterprise to even begin naming outstanding sites and authors. (No doubt, a new one has just popped up on the web this moment.)

Nevertheless…

- Phil Cubeta's *Gift Hub,* Beth Kanter's *Beth's Blog,* and Lucy Bernholz's *Philanthropy 2173* are websites that provide stimulating insights on a regular basis. Plus, they generously offer links to other thinkers and activists with fresh, vivid, and challenging ideas.

- I appreciate the instant online availability of tough-minded reports from the National Committee for Responsive Philanthropy and Grantmakers for Effective Organizations. To follow news, ongoing debates, and the usually civil exchange of ideas, I consult onPhilanthropy.com, the *Chronicle of Philanthropy*'s website, blog posts by affinity groups, and webzines published by regional grantmakers associations.

- When I want to learn about developments in the nonprofit sector, I turn to the online newsletter *Blue Avocado*, whose articles and analysis are consistently distinguished by clarity, imagination, and verve. In fact, Rick Cohen's coverage in *Blue Avocado* of the Vanguard Foundation's operatically tragic collapse recently set a high-water mark for philanthropic reporting—even as the regional and national media that should have investigated passed over the story glancingly.

Thanks to the energetic and largely uncompensated contributions of authors and bloggers throughout cyberspace, fledgling donors or experienced philanthropists can now profitably devote time regularly to exploring the web, studying, pondering opposing viewpoints, comparing visions of a world in flux. In the process, the context of philanthropy will grow ever more intriguing, as previously unavailable information and analysis tumbles across the screen.

The larger currents of the conversation are even leaking into the mainstream media. Over the past several years, *New York Times* columnist Nicholas Kristof has merged clear-eyed reporting with passionate advocacy for nonprofits working to alleviate poverty worldwide, often championing the "do-it-yourself foreign aid" of ordinary people linked up with like-minded donors. His columns and blog posts have drawn readers not otherwise versed in philanthropic lore to sites like *MYC4* for making business microloans to underwrite education worldwide. In a similar vein, social entrepreneurship expert David Bornstein (best known for his book *How to Change the World*) has teamed up with crack reporter and MacArthur Foundation Genius Award–winner Tina Rosenberg to cowrite *Fixes*, a *New York Times* blog that "looks at solutions to social problems and why they work"—a task many of us have longed to see skilled journalists undertake.

A decade of exponentially expanding connectivity has impressed upon most of us the enormous potential of intellectual exchange mediated by our desktop computers and handheld mobile devices. Today, the conversation is rich, varied, and barely begun.

Transparency Tech

Too many philanthropists have long held their cards close to their chests. Rudely put, their rationale boils down to *It's my money, and I'll do with it what I like.*

I'm not going to enumerate the small universe of problems larded into this particular line of thinking. Let me just say: It's wrong. Philanthropic dollars emerge in great profusion throughout American society because of the deal we've struck that enables donors to take tax write-offs for their contributions to the commonweal. Instead of taxing income at much higher rates to pay for government-sponsored services, we've grown a huge nonprofit sector supported by personal and institutional giving.

Would American philanthropy exist if the tax breaks evaporated? Certainly. Personal giving in support of the common good resides deep in the American character. Contrary to popular romance, the West was not "won" by ragtag bands of gunslinging individualists. (That's more a description of the sociopathic sliver of American character we're still coping with.) Rather, the material and moral progress of our nation derives from ordinary people who built new towns, founded public schools and universities, established standards and institutions for ensuring justice and order, helped one another when disaster struck, and pursued the communitarian impulse in countless ways great and small that have distinguished our country from its beginnings. This is all a rather roundabout way of saying that American philanthropy flourishes in the crucible of American cooperation. We all owe each other, all of the time.

But for the sake of argument, let's set aside the moral case. Simply on a pragmatic basis, there exists a compelling reason for donors to embrace transparency in their decision making and their actions:

It works.

I'll give you an example from our experience at the Packard Foundation.

A few years ago, our Conservation and Science Program was struggling to design a strategy for reducing agricultural nitrogen pollution, a leading cause of algal blooms and coastal dead zones in the oceans. Instead of exploring the issue exclusively in-house, or consulting privately with experts, we created an online forum—or wiki—and solicited advice from all interested parties. The wiki ran live for one month, attracting contributions from eighty-five participants whose ranks included climatologists, botanists, agronomists, government regulators, private industry leaders, and environmentalists.

Our request for help beyond our own institutional walls netted wide-ranging, high-caliber discussion and advice. Our staff deemed the input as useful as any conventional approach we might have undertaken, plus it attracted new voices. About half our contributors turned out to be people we previously had not known. We had tapped the wisdom of a small but knowledgeable crowd—one that could now work together on other issues. Ten years earlier, in the pre-wiki world, the tactic would have been unimaginable.

Technology is making transparency so much easier that it may eventually become a natural part of grantmaking—perhaps even obligatory.

An important step in that direction has been pioneered by the Foundation Center's Glasspockets initiative (www.glasspockets.org). Developed in partnership with the Center for Effective Philanthropy, the Communications Network, the Global Philanthropy Forum, Grantmakers for Effective Organizations, and the United Kingdom's One World Trust, Glasspockets offers essential facts about 97,000 US foundations and provides illustrations of philanthropy's impact on critical issues, such as climate change, health care, and poverty. It also highlights exemplary ways in which select foundations are embracing transparency, and it showcases the growing use of social media to speak to and learn from the vast world outside of organized philanthropy—with the initiative's *Transparency Talk* blog serving as a forum for the exchange of ideas and best practices. Furthermore, Glasspockets encourages foundations to speak frankly and publicly about their failures—something most foundations routinely urge their grantees to do, but seldom undertake in their own practice.

What do these efforts among foundations mean for individual donors? To begin, they could eventually make public a useful array of program strategies that individuals can select (or reject) in their own giving. They could point to nonprofit organizations making progress outside the glare of mainstream media. They could identify by name potential partners in forging funding alliances and leveraging their donations to far greater effect.

Most of all, they could set a new tone for giving in which openness, candor, and collaboration become expectations.

Of course, we may find that progress in these areas won't be urged forward by the major foundations. Rather, the innovations and leadership in transparency may be assumed by individual donors or the boards and staff of small activist foundations. By people whose personal and professional experience lead them to handle new tools with confidence and ease.

Dave Peery is a sterling example. In 2009, he launched a strategy session for his family foundation on Twitter, soliciting comments, ideas, and debate in real time from anybody who wanted to join the conversation. Although the foundation had existed for thirty years, the Twitter conference marked a new era in which a donor was asking the world how he and his family could best change the world. Twitter's evanescent quality seemed to encourage honesty, and its enforced brevity pointed the foundation to further reports, organizations, and individuals who in the near future could be tapped at length for advice. *Tactical Philanthropy* deemed it "a rather stunning form of transparency"—no doubt the first of its kind. But certainly not the last.

Acting Internationally

For most of its life, the Packard Foundation has invested considerable sums in projects outside of the United States. Our staff has traveled to China to help the world's fastest-growing economy reduce its energy footprint. We've partnered with environmentalists, farmers, and community leaders in Latin America and Indonesia to halt deforestation and spawn sustainable agricultural practices. We've joined health workers in Ethiopia, Pakistan, and Mexico to protect women's reproductive rights and improve care in sprawling cities and remote villages.

The Foundation enjoys a number of advantages that have allowed us to tackle these issues. We possess sufficient capital to launch ambitious initiatives. Our board is committed to supporting programs over many years until results can be charted and secured. Our program staff is recruited for its specialized knowledge, language skills, on-the-ground contacts, and extensive experience working abroad. Finally, our size and position in the foundation world affords our executive staff and board access to elected officials and in-country community leaders so that we can undertake the diplomatic efforts that so often prove a cornerstone of international philanthropy.

In other words, our institutional heft has allowed us to step upon the world stage with a confidence that individual donors could seldom match.

That's changed.

Today, individuals can employ a multitude of low-cost technologies that enable them to vastly reduce the costs and risks of participating in global philanthropy. The genius of Kiva, to take the best-known example, has been to aggregate small contributions from many donors worldwide and place them at the disposal of small-scale entrepreneurs in developing economies in the form of start-up low-interest loans. Kiva then partners with local agencies assisting the entrepreneurs and creates a feedback loop through these agencies and volunteer ambassadors, who visit funded projects and report back the results to donors via web video.

Unthinkable a dozen years ago. Today, it's almost routine, with increasing numbers of online nonprofit enterprises launching a variety of strategies that enable donors to loan, invest, or give away money that will underwrite a small business, seed a development project, or pay for the education of poor but ambitious students around the world. Donors can send their money globe-trotting on the wired wings of GlobalGiving, Global Greengrants Fund, Hope Equity, IDEX, the Virtual Foundation, Care2, Causes on Facebook, ChipIn, MicroGiving, TakingITGlobal, UniversalGiving, and more. In time, we're bound to see the leading activist sites become increasingly interconnected, providing donors with a simple means of locating outlets for their contributions of time, labor, or money—a global mash-up of all movements and metrics philanthropic. So you want to find the five leading organizations working to guarantee safe water resources in Central Asia? A few clicks and they appear on the screen. (Then it's up to you to choose among them—or better yet, dig deeper and determine how much of a commitment you want to make.) That's where we're heading, and probably quite soon.

Another important byproduct of international connectivity is an improved understanding of global needs.

"We've all seen situations," said a former Peace Corps volunteer, "where a person visits Africa and they're stunned by the beauty of the country, the graciousness of the people, and the desperate need they see everywhere. They tell themselves, 'I've got to do something.' But they don't really know what. Maybe they send over two containers filled with toys. Their heart is in the right place, but they haven't done their research. They need to study up, find out where there's a lack. They need to learn who they can team up with and how to leverage their personal contribution so they can make a real difference."

That's precisely what connectivity can do—and none too soon. While online giving in 2010 increased by a remarkable 35 percent (fueled partially by earthquake relief efforts in Haiti), less than 2 percent of all charitable giving in the United States travels abroad, most of that still dispersed by foundations. Governmental assistance also proves proportionately meager. Public surveys routinely find that Americans wildly overestimate the size of foreign aid—with many thinking the sum to constitute a quarter of the federal budget, when it actually lags around 1 percent.

Most of us must be considered wealthy in comparison to one billion of our fellow human beings. Indeed, over half of the world's population lives on less than two dollars per day—or about $700 a year.

The price of one inexpensive laptop.

The imbalance, and the opportunities, couldn't be clearer.

What to Do Instead of Drowning

Over the next several years, we stand to learn more than we ever could have imagined about what works in the social sector, and how to replicate, scale up, extend, and sustain our best efforts. The internet, text messaging, smart phones—and nameless new devices yet to be invented—will level the philanthropic playing field. They'll allow individuals (and more powerfully, individuals banding together, remotely and instantaneously) to tackle problems and carve out solutions once relegated to activist government and the big foundations. We're entering a world that's "causewired," to use Tom Watson's term (and the title of his terrific book on the subject). In a "causewired" world, global cross-talk leaps over, around, and through the institutional structures of philanthropy to engage ever more individuals in giving, volunteering, formulating ideas, and creating new institutions (including some that will pop up and then disappear in a flash).

No, technology won't change everything. If we imagine that it can substitute for all flesh-and-blood human contact, if it fastens us to our flat screens instead of flinging us out into the world, armed with better information and greater curiosity, if we find ourselves drowning in data, then it won't have changed enough.

But I don't think that's where we're heading. Rather, I see technology as a tool taking us places we could never have dreamed of going even a decade ago.

Almost certainly, we'll produce massive oceans of fresh data. Once charted and tamed so the logic and language of one enterprise can speak coherently to others—a mindboggling challenge now being undertaken by the better minds in our field—we'll be able to compare the impacts of various program strategies, identify the factors that make success in one region transportable to another, blend market-based solutions with nonprofit enterprise and government assistance, establish economies of scale, and vastly enlarge the realm of new donors. With greater ease, we'll be able to mine and export best practices within the nonprofit and philanthropic sectors. We'll be able to bind together advocacy at local, regional, national, and international levels. We'll tap wider audiences, stir appetites for civic participation, raise and satisfy increasingly ambitious expectations for change. We'll make collaboration feasible across borders and among disparate cultures and languages. We'll diminish the strains of endless fundraising by rationalizing applications and reports with consistent terms and categories, smoothing the way for comparison, measurement, and analysis—and hurrying money into the hands of those who will put it to best use. We'll be able to wring the answers from questions we can't even pose now because the data churned up by wave after wave of previous data hasn't yet delivered them to our door.

Of course, it's still up to us to manage the hard slog of getting to where we want to go, day after day. But technology will almost certainly point us in the right direction, illuminate multiple pathways, and help us reach our destination of a freer, fairer, and more beautiful world.

7

Making Generosity Contagious

Principle #7 *Change the culture.*

When Lisa Parker turned fourteen, her father told her that he had to make a trip to Romania. After the fall of the Ceauşescu dictatorship, terrible stories had begun to circulate about the fate of Romanian orphans. As a physician board member of the Catholic Health Association, he had been asked to investigate.

"He was devastated by what he found," remembered Lisa. "We had heard about the warehousing of children, but the actual conditions turned out to be horrific. All ages held in metal cribs with no mattresses, banging their heads against the bars. Some had diapers, others didn't—you can imagine the smells. Everybody was malnourished. Nobody touched them. Dad asked a staffer for a particular child's name. 'Oh,' she said, 'they don't have names.'"

When Lisa's father returned, he spoke to everybody who would listen, insisting that their faith and common decency demanded they take action. Nobody disagreed, but other matters always seemed to come first.

"Finally," remembered Lisa, "Dad pulled out his own checkbook. 'I'm writing the first check to the Nameless Children of Romania Fund,' he said.

From that point, he went back often. His experience there became central to his life."

Over the years, the Fund built eight children's homes run by Romanian staff. It established a rehabilitation unit in the state children's hospital in Bucharest and provided equipment and training for the physical therapists with the understanding that at least half the patients would be orphanage residents. The Fund also equipped Romania's first facility for the education of children with Down syndrome, and paid its staff salaries.

As a teenager, Lisa was shaken by the horror stories of postcommunist Romania. She had grown up in a loving, stable family blessed by relative affluence and the expectation of civic stability. Now, at the dinner table, she began to perceive the suffering and turmoil that plagued much of the world. She also recognized the everyday heroism of her father—a man who took action when others seemed stymied by the magnitude of needs and the effort required to meet them.

"The first Thanksgiving after Dad went to Romania, we were all sitting around the table and he was going to say the prayer. He just sobbed. He wasn't an emotionally effusive person. But he kept repeating that he couldn't get over how lucky we all were. Him sitting there with his children and grandkids. Food at the table."

When Lisa's father contracted pancreatic cancer in 2002—managing to live another three years, although his initial diagnosis gave him only three months—his sense of gratitude and responsibility only increased.

"He was charged with this amazing spirit," said Lisa. "He felt that every person who touched his life was a blessing, every day a gift. You didn't leave his presence without knowing that he loved you. It was a great lesson for all of us. Dad said that his last three years were the best of his life. The stuff that really matters was all that mattered now."

We all learn how to live from our families. The example of our parents, their parents, our aunts and uncles and even our siblings, all contribute mightily to our sense of the world and our place in it. They predict to an extraordinary degree whether we will reach out with courage and generosity when facing adversity and want, or fearfully retract in a futile effort to insulate ourselves from the trials of life and the necessity of acting boldly.

For Lisa, her family's example proved hugely persuasive, seeding her own early interest in philanthropy. But the familial influence didn't end with her father's pro bono medical work and international activism. She also learned about giving alongside her mother, who worked as a foundation executive. Starting in her early teens, Lisa frequently accompanied her on site visits to nonprofits throughout Southern California.

"We went to Proyecto Pastoral," she recalled. "It was started by Father Greg Boyle, who later founded Homeboy Industries—the group that's worked so successfully with gang members. We visited Father Boyle's parish because he'd requested funding for a homeless men's shelter that served recent migrants who spent their days searching for work. They got a bed, shower, food, a post office box. He took us around the operation and described his vision for a childcare co-op and school to serve the men's families. Over the years, these things came to fruition, along with his determination to crack the gang problem. For me, as a young person, it just penetrated. There's no substitute for being there. Reading the grant proposal is a pale reflection of reality. It got deep into me because I could see it, hear it, feel it."

This on-the-ground experience prepared Lisa to participate at an early age in her family's foundation. As children and teens, she and her cousins convened a "junior board" that ran their own meetings, studied grant proposals, conducted site visits, championed their own issues, and ultimately determined where 10 percent of the budget would be spent. Encouraged then to sit in on the full board's meetings and participate fully, Lisa now acknowledges that initially she didn't realize that she was still in training and wouldn't have a vote on policies (and the destination of the other 90 percent of grant dollars) until she reached adulthood.

"What mattered," she emphasized, "was the experience of being respected in the boardroom. We thought that our voice counted and we could make a difference. There's no greater feeling than realizing that you have something worthwhile to offer. When I had my own kids, it became urgent for me to get them involved. My daughter was only three days old, and I was wondering *Now how do I get her interested in giving?* Over the years, I took our children to do volunteer work at the local animal shelter and community garden. I wanted to normalize service as a part of life. I spent the next decade looking at how to nurture that impulse in kids at every developmental stage."

These days, Lisa serves as an advisor to wealthy families and their financial planners ("who usually don't know where to start when it comes to kids' giving"). "My goal is to help them raise citizen philanthropists. It doesn't matter how much money a person has. I want to light up kids about the process of giving. That's what many wealthy parents want. They hate to see their children consumed by consumerism. It's heartbreaking. But if you wait until they're thirty to get them involved, that's what's probably going to happen."

As a board member, Lisa has also come full circle at her own family foundation—now serving as a mentor and prime example of an engaged giver for the younger members. Each year, she organizes a philanthropy camp for the next generation, deemed Cousinpalooza. Most recently, fourteen children drawn from Lisa's family's fourth philanthropic generation, aged four through nineteen, gathered in San Diego to attend presentations by local nonprofits. Then they spread out across the region to volunteer with the organizations and learn about the issues in practice. At end of their gathering, they met once again to decide how to allocate $5,000. The foundation matched each of their grants.

"Interesting conversations come up as the kids are trying to decide what to fund," said Lisa. "They discover they have different convictions. One's really passionate about child soldiers in Uganda. Another is keen on the environment and she argues that the child soldiers won't survive if the world's burning up. The process exposes them to a variety of issues—how else can they learn what they care about? They're pitting need against need, making priorities—perhaps for the first time in their lives. I'm amazed by their sophistication. One adult is always present to answer questions, but the kids choose their own facilitator and work through everything together. It drives home the point that it doesn't have to just be adults around the board table making a difference."

Next-Generation Philanthropy

A familial emphasis on giving is a kind of capital investment. Like education, it offers lifelong rewards. For some, it can be an opening to a career; for others, an avocational ticket to adventure. For all of us, empathy and generosity provide a means to productively enter the world with our hearts wide open. And don't forget all that research regarding the bounce-back effects of everyday altruism. As Albert Schweitzer declared long before the advent of longitudinal studies and laboratory brain scans of generous individuals: "The only ones among you who will be really happy are those who will have sought and found how to serve." Persistent, thoughtful giving and engagement with others is a dependable path to a satisfying life. Do we want anything less for our children?

Beyond the powerful example of parental commitment and action, what else do kids need to spark their own interest in philanthropy?

From an early age, kids need to understand *why* we give. They need context and clarity about the purpose of philanthropy, and the conditions in the world that make it necessary. They need to enter the discussion, no matter how tentatively at first, about the myriad ways in which involvement in community life can bring us meaning, dignity, and purpose. When we talk in concrete terms about the use of our time, talent, and treasure to help people outside our own family, we inevitably ignite the imaginations of the young—particularly if we start the conversation early. As usual, they'll have a million questions. And that's precisely the point. We'll all gain from trying to grapple with their curiosity about the motivations and authenticity of our own giving.

Beyond our personal stories, we can point out to our kids how many of the institutions and experiences they cherish result from someone else's generosity, be it contributions of money or time and effort. That park they enjoy playing in: say thanks to the taxpayers who approved the bond issue covering the costs. The soccer team and Little League: impossible without volunteer coaches, referees, and after-game groundskeepers. The family dog? A volunteer rescue organization found and fed her, and then made certain she had the right home for her continuing care and contentment. We live in a highly associative society that can only survive by the renewed commitment of each successive generation to the commonweal. Children need to grasp the dimensions of our public sphere long before they can conceptualize its complex dynamics or engage in the long-running debate about its funding and future.

Finally, kids have to get their hands dirty. Unlike Lisa, most won't have two parents steeped in philanthropy. But even children raised in the most avidly philanthropic families must still forge their own paths to personal giving.

Fortunately, one of the most heartening developments in recent years has been the proliferation of giving programs aimed at and frequently directed by young people.

- YouthGive.org is an outstanding example of the new movement. Its web presence enables children and teenagers to open a secure online giving account and then direct support to a variety of projects that have been researched by other young people and vetted by their families, schools, and community organizations. In many ways, YouthGive reflects the promise of a new generation of young philanthropists. Their cadres instinctively embrace technology to propagate their mission, think "glocally" (that is, both globally and locally), and collaborate with their peers in communal efforts instead of replicating the longstanding individualist approach to giving.

- In Michigan, the state's community foundations, allied with the W.K. Kellogg Foundation, have spawned eighty-six permanently endowed youth funds, matched by more than $100 million raised at the local level. The funds are overseen by Youth Advisory Committees charged with grantmaking to address issues of special concern to young people. Every summer, Youth Advisory Committee members come together in a conference with their advisors and young donors from other states to strategize methods for extending their reach and effectiveness. Other states have launched similar programs.

- Independent associations, such as New Global Citizens, match young people with nonprofits and nongovernmental organizations around the world. As intermediaries to service agencies, they assist young people with expanding community awareness about critical problems and raising money for grassroots solutions "where a small investment of resources makes a tremendous impact on the project community."

- The Foundation Center now allocates a portion of its website to Youth in Philanthropy. The pages are richly cached with personal stories of young philanthropists and links to get beginners involved.

A decade ago, research indicated over three hundred youth and high school philanthropy programs operating in the United States—along with complementary efforts in eight other countries. Today, evidence suggests that growth in this area has continued, thanks to the proliferation of new technologies that spread the tools of youth giving worldwide. It's a trend that adults should take seriously and aid whenever possible. In fact, I'd like to see foundations jump into the business of assisting youth philanthropies on a state and local basis—providing a bit of capital, tools, training, and perhaps some discreet guidance when necessary. The young people will take over from there. In the process of accomplishing good work around the globe, they'll be readying themselves to assume leadership roles in philanthropy and nonprofit service with skills and experience their parents never dreamed of.

Talking about Giving

Generosity should be contagious. Amid the intimacy of the family circle or within groups of youthful peers, it almost can't help spreading.

But what about the rest of us? Does our own public face reflect our commitment to philanthropy? Where and when do we articulate our vision of an interdependent world nourished by the discipline of thoughtful giving?

In truth, the national conversation about philanthropy is largely conducted in whispers. I have to agree with Bill Somerville when he says that "most Americans don't know the first thing about philanthropy."

"Then again," as Bill argues in his book *Grassroots Philanthropy*, "how could they? Not a single mass-market print journalist is assigned a full-time beat to cover the foundation world. Television reporting remains negligible—at best, reduced to announcements of ambitious funding initiatives sponsored by the larger institutions. (At worst, broadcasters periodically trot out minute-long teasers about some local funder who may have wandered awry of its fiscal responsibilities.) From the great stages of public life—the governor's mansion, the Senate, the White House—we almost never hear a knowledgeable word uttered about philanthropy's practices, problems, or promise (except perhaps to announce that the government is pulling out of the business of funding this or that enterprise, and it will now be up to foundations to pick up the slack....) Altogether, it's a mind-boggling omission. Despite our size, wealth, influence, and potential, philanthropy is absent from the national conversation."

Of course, Bill is speaking about private foundations, a world which puzzles most people outside of the field. But I also think those of us who embrace philanthropy as a personal value—individuals who give regularly, even substantially—bear some of the responsibility for the conversation that's not taking place. Our collective voice is potentially thunderous. Yet we remain mute.

I want to make a radical proposal: Let's start talking about our personal giving with our friends.

Yes, I recognize the pitfalls…

We'll sound like braggarts. Or scolds. Or sanctimonious, dewy-eyed do-gooders.

Or worse.

But think about what we sacrifice by remaining silent.

We forfeit the wisdom and counsel of friends and colleagues who might sharpen our perceptions and improve the effectiveness of our giving. We ignore an essential aspect of our humanity, forgetting that altruism is an essential building block of civilization. We miss out on any number of rousing good discussions and debates.

Most important, we lose the opportunity to publicly affirm the importance of philanthropy and therefore bring influence to bear on the rest of society. We contain our experience and insight within the single cell of our own being, when it might very well blossom and reseed the world.

I realize that many generous people don't think of themselves as *philanthropists*. It's a clunky word, anyway. (Too many syllables derived from ancient Greek: *philos,* meaning love, tied to *anthropy,* or mankind. "Love for humanity.") No wonder we balk. It all sounds a bit pious, smug, and self-congratulatory. (It also confuses. Some years ago, funding advocates hit the streets of Los Angeles and questioned bypassers about the meaning of the word. They found an alarming number of citizens who think philanthropy has something to do with stamp collecting or the study of skull shapes.) We could benefit from a replacement term carved out in short, stout Anglo-Saxon. But we don't have one. "Donor" will have to do. Philanthropy is the etymological cross we all have to bear.

So let's do it.

Let's make public our philanthropic actions and illuminate the rationale backing them up. At least, let's do so in the company of trusted companions. It's a sad truth that we're more likely to hear the salacious details of a near-stranger's recent divorce than the sound logic underlying our closest friends' annual giving plans. I'm not advocating that we turn tales of our personal generosity into a big brouhaha. (Now there's a word.) Rather, we can introduce into polite conversation our experience with *trying* to be effective donors. We can discuss the struggle. Our doubts. Our imperfect aim and the equivocal results. The kind of victories that encourage us to keep giving. The kind of world that we're aiming to build. Our fears for the future, our hopes for our children and grandchildren—and the best means we've discovered so far for advancing justice, beauty, and abundance. These are all topics worthy of authentic adult conversation. Approached with honesty and zest, they can at least help us come to know one another on far more intimate terms than polite chatter normally allows.

I like to imagine a small circle of friends passing time around the fireplace on a wintry evening. (Somehow this sounds more compelling than a network of virtual colleagues gathered together in some cozy chat room on the web.) Then somebody stirs up the coals of conversation by raising a few of the questions that reside behind the philanthropic impulse:

- How has giving changed the way you look at the world?

- What acts of kindness and generosity are you most proud of?

- What do you wish you could do for others if you had greater resources? More important, what can you do now that you haven't yet begun with the resources presently at your disposal?

No, it's not a typical American conversation. But with a light touch, it could become a more common one. Our consumer society encourages us to feel greater reticence about expressing our need to give than selfishly asserting the urge to keep taking. At the same time, the constant promise of *more*—be it goods, wealth, or security—tamps down our gratitude for what we already possess. We have to be conscious of these forces. In the end, however, I don't believe that it's just rampant consumerism that undermines honest talk about giving. Rather, it's something deeper and more daunting. At the heart of this conversation resides the most serious of all inquiries:

What are you going to do with the remaining capital of your life?

For some individuals, the answer might be change spouses, go on a cruise, blow the rest of the money in some lavish fashion so the kids can't squander it later. But for many others, the question can elicit life-shaking consideration.

Thoughtful philanthropy is a forge in which character may be formed or reformed at any age. If life hasn't maimed our better instincts, we often long to make significant contributions in our later years as the palpable manifestation of accumulated experience and wisdom. Not to do so isn't just selfish. It suggests an inability to nourish what's deep and necessary in our own psyches.

But generosity doesn't just benefit donors and the vast nonprofit sector. It also builds better citizens.

In his book *Who Really Cares*, Arthur C. Brooks argues that "people who give are far more likely to be active political participants than people who do not give." According to data culled from the 2000 Social Capital Community Benchmark Survey and 2004 Maxwell Poll, donors or volunteers were more than twice as likely as others to attend a political meeting, participate in a political group, or belong to a group taking local action for political reform. Members of voluntary associations were 16 percentage points more likely to say they followed public affairs, 25

Popping the Question

Many people feel an urge to contribute. They're looking for something to do that will add another layer of meaning to their daily lives and put into balance an overabundance of privilege and material goods. But they can't necessarily articulate these drives. Indeed, they may even be immersed in lives of civic contribution but not realize it—until somebody poses the clarifying question.

One active donor makes a practice out of changing the conversation in ways that shine a light on the secret life of everyday philanthropy—and honor the unsung and often unexpressed contributions of ordinary people.

"Whenever I'm in a cab or waiting to check in at a hotel desk or when I meet somebody new," she said, "I'll often ask them what they're doing with their volunteer time. How they're contributing to their local community. What they're proudest of in terms of their efforts. Who they give to and which nonprofits they support. I end up learning about lots of efforts I never would have heard about otherwise, and we end up talking about the things that really matter. We become more real to each other. We remind ourselves that we are all in the same boat, we all have to pull together—and in many different ways, that's just what we're doing."

points more likely to vote, and 26 points more likely to contact their elected officials in a given year.

If giving is a bulwark of democracy, then talking about giving may be the prerequisite to bolder, more capacious philanthropy at every level.

"You can't start a movement in philanthropy if you don't have a conversation about giving among ordinary people," said longtime activist

Ron Rowell. "We have to inspire one another to believe that we can join together and create the kind of world we want to live in. Believing that's possible is the hardest part. But over time, many little conversations begin to form a pool of interest that eventually can be harnessed into the power of a wave. Once you start talking with others, you see how much difference giving can make in the world—and not incidentally, in your own life."

Over three hundred years ago, John Bunyan put it nicely in *The Pilgrim's Progress*:

"A man there was, though some did count him mad,

the more he cast away the more he had."

Asking the Big Questions

A donor well known for her support of social justice causes took a friend to see a dance performance in New York. After the final curtain, she confided that she had recently joined the board of directors to deal with the dance company's perennial deficit.

"I see," responded her friend. "You've gotten disillusioned with politics."

The donor sighed. It was the kind of comment she had grown to expect.

"It doesn't have to be either/or," the donor later explained. "They're not opposed. If anything, they're connected. I see the arts as a way of telling us where we're heading as a society. Artists can point out what we may not want to see. It's vision that makes them artists in the first place and enables them to serve as our society's freest voices. We need those qualities."

I'm sympathetic to this point of view. But I don't think it actually goes far enough. For decades now, arts advocates have sustained a valiant effort to justify public funding and private donations from the ramparts of every imaginable rationale. They cite research demonstrating that training in the arts keeps kids in school, minimizes behavior problems, and reduces the likelihood of teen pregnancy. They argue that students proficient in performing and visual arts test higher in math and reading than their uninitiated peers. They point to communities once on the brink of collapse that have been rescued by philanthropic investments in dance, music, and theater companies, with every dollar spent on tickets to a performing arts event generating five dollars for local businesses.

Yet the skepticism remains. Can we afford the arts any longer given the fiscal crisis in our city/state/nation? Should we direct our limited dollars to a pursuit that doesn't house, feed, or cure anybody when all these desperate needs stare us in the face daily? Can't the artists and their audiences cover the costs—particularly since everybody onstage and off seems to be enjoying themselves so much?

Of course, artists will continue to make art regardless of donor support. They always have, and let's hope they always will. But as a society, we have a responsibility to pay our fair share for the myriad benefits derived from the artists' largely unsubsidized efforts. The case is easily made that artists themselves are the primary donors to our diverse and dynamic culture— at least, in terms of years dedicated over lifetimes to learning, practicing, presenting, and teaching the arts. Philanthropy can't take us even halfway to meeting their contribution. We are always in their debt. And the debt is enormous.

"In an age of suspicion and fear," said Ben Cameron, program director at the Doris Duke Charitable Foundation and one of the nation's most eloquent advocates for cultural funding, "arts are an invitation to regard one another with curiosity and generosity." To my mind, that's sufficient reason alone to back them generously.

But how?

"Choose one living artist to support in your lifetime," said a philanthropist well versed in the arts' virtues. "That's what I tell my friends these days. You give them the means to accomplish their work, and they'll do the rest."

One ingenious vehicle for supporting individual artists has been the annual grants awarded to women artists at midcareer by Anonymous Was a Woman. (The organization's name is taken from *A Room of One's Own*, Virginia Woolf's classic indictment of the social and material forces aligned against the work and recognition of women artists.) To date, more than 150 women have received "no strings" grants of $25,000 to pay for studio space, materials, equipment, documentation, catalogs, and the inestimable gift of time to work. Begun in 1995, after the National Endowment for the Arts dropped its individual artist fellowships following a partisan uproar over several recipients, Anonymous Was a Woman emerged as the brain-child of a New York artist who has herself managed to remain nameless over two decades—as have the art historians, curators, writers, and previous winners who submit the nominations.

It's a neat model that deserves widespread replication. A bevy of national, regional, and even citywide fellowships in all the arts would make cultural life richer throughout our nation. It would also provide some needed balance to the activities and vocations we publicly honor. Not just sports heroes, movie stars, and outlandish tycoons, but also first-chair symphony oboists, fledgling photographers, and dancers sailing from tap to modern to ballet.

On a larger scale, we can also invest much more in grassroots arts organizations. I'm speaking here of the relatively small, largely uncelebrated arts centers that enliven our communities while cultivating the artists and audiences of tomorrow. Sad to say, the once-vital national infrastructure of community arts groups, aligned with innovative state funding agencies, a healthy National Endowment for the Arts and National Endowment for the Humanities, and a visionary federal/local jobs program for artists run through the Comprehensive Employment Training Act (CETA) has now all but vanished. Support for painting, music, drama, and filmmaking—particularly in poor and working-class communities—has been increasingly left to individual initiative. On the walls of our state and federal legislatures, one can easily read the cramped and unsightly scrawl: *No funding increases for years to come....*It's up to donors to pick up the slack (while taking whatever political measures feasible to loosen civic purse strings).

I bring up the issue of arts funding not just because I am a supporter of the arts. I am—for all the reasons I've mentioned and more. And I'm particularly proud of the Packard Foundation's efforts over several decades to keep music education alive in the public schools. But my concern for the arts' future in America also reflects my interest in a much larger question—one that individual donors must ask themselves at every turn:

What kind of a world do we want to leave behind?

Are we content with a tuneless hodgepodge of commercial bunk in which the authentic pursuit of beauty and truth is deemed mere fluff or an elitist pastime? "When I hear the word culture, I reach for my gun"—that's the telling line commonly attributed to Nazi henchmen Hermann Göring or Heinrich Himmler. (Actually, it comes from an obscure piece of Third Reich theatrical propaganda.) I prefer the sly Gallic revision by director Jean-Luc Godard. In his 1963 film *Contempt*, Godard has one character inform another famous auteur: "Whenever I hear the word culture, I bring out my checkbook."

The arts is just one area that demands audacious generosity, openness, and the willingness to move against the prevailing current.

Take the matter of taxes. Our present system of taxation has been central to the growth of both our nonprofit and philanthropic sectors. It's also a system rife with inequities and incapable of sustaining many of the institutions and activities that we value. In the words of grassroots fundraising expert Kim Klein: "How many times have we found ourselves saying, 'As a nonprofit we do more with less.' If we continue this approach without challenging the status quo, we'll end up doing very little with next to nothing."

Unexpectedly, we've benefitted from the powerful advocacy of a few wealthy individuals, such as Chuck Collins and Bill Gates, Sr., who have argued that the estate tax should be renamed the Gratitude Tax in recognition of the publicly funded universities, highways, scientific research centers, health and safety inspectors, and all the other government-supported institutions and programs that have made the abundant creation of wealth possible in America. As Warren Buffett once responded to an interviewer's query about his famous investing prowess: "If you stick me down in the middle of Bangladesh or Peru or someplace, you'll find out how much this talent is going to produce in the wrong kind of soil. I will be struggling thirty years later."

Some things philanthropy can't do. Civilization requires collective effort, civic commitment. "You can give a poor family a box of food when they're hungry," asserted Philip Arca, executive director for St. Vincent de Paul of Alameda County. "But as an individual, no matter how wealthy, you can't provide them with a system for health care, education, or a job that supports them with dignity."

Those are tasks we have to take on together as citizens and voters, as well as philanthropists.

Our work begins by acknowledging the limits of personal giving—and then applying all our might to pushing our society in the direction of greater equity and opportunity by every means at our disposal. This requires us to approach our civic and philanthropic responsibilities not as opposing but as complementary forces—applying to each our utmost seriousness, ingenuity, and enthusiasm. It compels us to recognize that engaged giving is both a duty and joy.

Working today as citizen-philanthropists to help make a more beautiful, bounteous, and fairer future is the privilege of a lifetime.

Epilogue

Seven Proposals for More Powerful Giving

1. Give more to what you care about most—and give first.
Ask yourself: *What changes do I want to see in the world over the next five years? The next ten or twenty-five?* Recognize the kinds of efforts that fire your imagination and stir your heart, and back them up with grants of significant size. Occasionally stretch your contributions past the usual comfort point. When you find a promising effort that's yet to secure funding, be the first to give. Then trumpet your commitment to other funders who might follow your lead.

2. Provide general operating support over multiple years.
Help nonprofits pursue their missions by negotiating dependable, no-strings grants over five years or more. Give an organization discretionary money to cover the administration of your favorite programs, along with plant maintenance, technology, fundraising, and all the other expenditures that most foundations, government agencies, and individual donors don't want to pay for. Collaborate with the nonprofit staff and board to plan for

your eventual withdrawal, and then recruit new donors to compensate for your absence before the time comes to leave.

3. Tap intermediaries to reach places you'll never go.

Acknowledge the limitations of your own personal experience, and seek out individuals and organizations to locate good funding investments in unfamiliar territories. Fund knowledgeable and practiced grantmaking organizations, such as the Funding Exchange and Women's Funding Network, that possess deep, reliable experience in the communities you most want to help.

4. Include "risky" grants in your mix.

Vary your philanthropic portfolio with judicious support for promising but untested organizations. Give some portion of your money to international efforts. Back groups who have trouble attracting funds because their work challenges the status quo. Aid individuals who are making a difference outside the conventional nonprofit structure. Pay attention to your fears and let them guide you towards useful, challenging grantmaking.

5. Improve your philanthropic skills.

Cultivate experienced mentors and learn from them over the years. Study the issues, develop specialties, and keep abreast of improved tools and strategies for giving. Join a giving circle and learn from the wisdom of a small, committed crowd. Help new donors learn the ropes as you gain insight and skill.

6. Embrace creative technology.

Use technology in the spirit of opening doors and forging new connections. Find the emerging means to facilitate conversation and transparency, extend philanthropic reach, and improve your effectiveness as a donor. Help nonprofits build their own technology capacities.

7. Create a culture of giving.

Encourage young people to engage in giving time and money to the causes they value. Assist philanthropic organizations founded and run by young people. Talk with your friends about why and how you all give. Stand up for the collective efforts that make our world more beautiful, bounteous, and just. Take joy in giving, and spread the feeling.

About the Authors

Colburn Wilbur is a trustee and former president of the David and Lucile Packard Foundation. He was the CEO of the Foundation for twenty-three years, from 1976 to 1999. During this period, he oversaw the Foundation's growth from a one-person staff and $500,000 in annual grantmaking to an $11 billion foundation with a staff of over 150 awarding over $400 million a year in four major program areas. Now, as a trustee, he is active in support of the Foundation's environmental initiatives, including work in building philanthropy in China and encouraging smart growth and energy conservation by Chinese policy makers.

Prior to joining the Packard Foundation, Cole served as executive director and CEO of the Sierra Club Foundation. He also worked in international banking and managed a computer service bureau.

Cole was a senior fellow at the Council on Foundations (1999–2000), and in 1999 received COF's Distinguished Grantmaker Award. He has been an active member of COF's Family Philanthropy Program and has served on a number of committees. Cole was COF's interim president and CEO in 2005.

In addition to serving on the Packard Foundation Board, Cole is currently a member of the boards of Colorado College, the Institute for Global Ethics, Planned Parenthood Mar Monte, the Stanford Theatre, and the Philanthropic Ventures Foundation. He is on the steering committee of the National Network of Consultants to Grantmakers and a number of advisory boards.

Cole received both his undergraduate and MBA degrees from Stanford University and is the coauthor of *The Complete Guide to Grantmaking Basics*.

Fred Setterberg is the coauthor of several books about the nonprofit sector and philanthropy, including *The Complete Guide to Grantmaking Basics,* with Colburn Wilbur and Barbara Kibbe; *Grassroots Philanthropy,* with Bill Somerville; and *Beyond Profit,* with Kary Schulman.

About Heyday

Heyday is an independent, nonprofit publisher and unique cultural institution. We promote widespread awareness and celebration of California's many cultures, landscapes, and boundary-breaking ideas. Through our well-crafted books, public events, and innovative outreach programs we are building a vibrant community of readers, writers, and thinkers.

Thank You

It takes the collective effort of many to create a thriving literary culture. We are thankful to all the thoughtful people we have the privilege to engage with. Cheers to our writers, artists, editors, storytellers, designers, printers, bookstores, critics, cultural organizations, readers, and book lovers everywhere!

We are especially grateful for the generous funding we've received for our publications and programs during the past year from foundations and hundreds of individual donors. Major supporters include:

Acorn Naturalists; Alliance for California Traditional Artists; Anonymous; James J. Baechle; Bay Tree Fund; Barbara Jean and Fred Berensmeier; Joan Berman; Buena Vista Rancheria; Lewis and Sheana Butler; California Civil Liberties Public Education Program, California State Library; California Council for the Humanities; The Keith Campbell Foundation; Center for California Studies; City of Berkeley; Compton Foundation; Lawrence Crooks; Nik Dehejia; Frances Dinkelspiel; Troy Duster; Euclid Fund at the East Bay Community Foundation; Mark and Tracy Ferron; Judith Flanders; Karyn and Geoffrey Flynn; Furthur Foundation; The Fred Gellert Family Foundation; Wallace Alexander Gerbode Foundation; Nicola W. Gordon; Wanda

Lee Graves and Stephen Duscha; Alice Guild; Walter & Elise Haas Fund; Coke and James Hallowell; Hawaii Sons, Inc.; Sandra and Charles Hobson; G. Scott Hong Charitable Trust; Kendeda Fund; Marty and Pamela Krasney; Kathy Kwan and Robert Eustace; Guy Lampard and Suzanne Badenhoop; LEF Foundation; Kermit Lynch Wine Merchant; Michael McCone; Michael J. Moratto, in memory of Ernest L. Cassel; Steven Nightingale; Pacific Legacy, Inc.; Patagonia, Inc.; John and Frances Raeside; Redwoods Abbey; Robin Ridder; Alan Rosenus; The San Francisco Foundation; San Manuel Band of Mission Indians; Tom Sargent; Sonoma Land Trust; Martha Stanley; Roselyne Chroman Swig; Thendara Foundation; Sedge Thomson and Sylvia Brownrigg; Tides Foundation; TomKat Charitable Trust; The Roger J. and Madeleine Traynor Foundation; Marion Weber; White Pine Press; John Wiley & Sons, Inc.; The Dean Witter Foundation; Lisa Van Cleef and Mark Gunson; and Yocha Dehe Wintun Nation.

Board of Directors

Getting Involved

To learn more about our publications, events, membership club, and other ways you can participate, please visit www.heydaybooks.com.